Prepared by the Special Publications Division
National Geographic Society, Washington, D. C.

The

Craftsman in America

The Craftsman in America

Contributing Authors
CLAY ANDERSON, ANDY LEON HARNEY,
  TOM MELHAM, CYNTHIA RUSS RAMSAY,
  PATRICIA L. RAYMER, BEVERLY SPOTSWOOD,
  C. MALCOLM WATKINS

Published by
THE NATIONAL GEOGRAPHIC SOCIETY
MELVIN M. PAYNE, *President*
MELVILLE BELL GROSVENOR, *Editor-in-Chief*
GILBERT M. GROSVENOR, *Editor*

Prepared by
THE SPECIAL PUBLICATIONS DIVISION
ROBERT L. BREEDEN, *Editor*
DONALD J. CRUMP, *Associate Editor*
PHILIP B. SILCOTT, *Senior Editor*
MARY ANN HARRELL, *Managing Editor*
JENNIFER URQUHART, NANCY W. GLASER,
  TEE LOFTIN SNELL, *Research*

Illustrations
BATES LITTLEHALES, *Picture Editor*
RONALD M. FISHER, WILLIAM R. GRAY, P. TYRUS
  HARRINGTON, TOM MELHAM, CYNTHIA RUSS
  RAMSAY, *Picture Legends*

Design and Art Direction
JOSEPH A. TANEY, *Staff Art Director*
JOSEPHINE B. BOLT, *Art Director*
URSULA PERRIN, *Assistant Art Director*
JANE D'ALELIO, *Design Assistant*

Production and Printing
ROBERT W. MESSER, *Production Manager*
GEORGE V. WHITE, *Assistant Production Manager*
RAJA D. MURSHED, NANCY W. GLASER, *Production
  Assistants*
JOHN R. METCALFE, *Engraving and Printing*
MARY G. BURNS, JANE H. BUXTON, STEPHANIE S.
  COOKE, NATALIE IGLITZ, SUZANNE J. JACOBSON,
  SANDRA LEE MATTHEWS, SELINA PATTON,
  MARILYN L. WILBUR, KAREN G. WILSON, *Staff
  Assistants*
ANNE K. MCCAIN, BARBARA L. KLEIN, *Index*

Library of Congress ⊂⫐⊃ Data: page 199

*Overleaf: In the cabinetmaker's shop at Old Sturbridge
Village, Massachusetts, R.E. Bushnell turns a handle on
a reproduction lathe of a type used in the early
Republic. Page 1: Hungarian-born woodcarver William
Thallmayer of Waukesha, Wisconsin, shapes an American
eagle. Endpaper: Appliqué quilt by Phoebe Cook, dated
1872, depicts her neighbors at Mount Gilead, Ohio.*

OVERLEAF: N.G.S. PHOTOGRAPHER BATES LITTLEHALES; PAGE 1:
LOWELL GEORGIA; HARD COVER ADAPTED FROM A PHOTOGRAPH
BY LOWELL GEORGIA.

*Craftwork of two traditions suggests the
complexity of the American heritage. A
buckskin autobiography painted about
1875 records exploits of a Cheyenne
warrior in battle. A silver medal—
commissioned by Congress, engraved by
hand, and issued in quantity—portrays the
first President and an Indian chief
sharing the pipe of peace. Government
officials presented such medals to in-
fluential Indians as tokens of friendship.*

Foreword

EVERY MORNING when I dress for work, I smile smugly at the quiet, smooth way my chest of drawers opens and closes at a slight touch of a fingertip. The early sun's rays reflect the warm matched grain and the rich color of the wood. My pleasure goes beyond mere ownership, for I built that chest myself from teak I imported from Burma and carefully aged in my basement workshop for two years.

Every hobbyist shares my feeling, whether he or she works in wood, metal, or fiber. Each time we utilize the object we have made, we revisit all its satisfactions. The sensation goes far beyond pride to the very wellsprings of human identity.

And well it should, for crafts and tools and homely arts launched humanity on the road toward civilization. Today I think they keep us there. Certainly I know of no better restorative than the hours I spend among fragrant wood shavings at my own carpenter's bench. I am away from every distraction and far from the world's disorders. While I work, I can see my hands give wood a form and shape and *use*. The satisfaction is intense.

In the same spirit we present this book, not so much a how-to as a how-come. We see here the essence of the American experience. And its amazing, wide-screen variety: from Eastern shipwrights to Navajo weavers, from those who work with needles to those who work with sledgehammers, from saddlemakers and banjo-builders to the potter who's "always praying over the kiln." No wonder that today Americans are turning away from this age of molded plastic, that city-dwellers are joining their country cousins in a phenomenal renaissance of native crafts.

Here we see a wide sampling of their one-of-a-kind work. To me, the photographs here are downright subversive: I'm tempted to try half a dozen new ideas in my own basement.

Why *not* try some metalwork? And why not try some of those sailor's knots that turn into macramé? Or block-printing? How I admire Arlinka Blair's work that adorns my living-room wall—and now appears in this book.

This volume inspires feelings of admiration and competition. It's less like a catalogue and more like a county fair. The difference, of course, is *people*.

"You can't be bored with your work," observes textile artist Lenore Tawney. "Because if you are bored, you put that boredom into the fiber, it stays there, becomes a part of that work."

Crafts have that special human investment. And perhaps something more.

"Wood has had a life of its own," notes Ohio sculptor David Hostetler. He works in bronze and stone—"But wood always draws me back; it's a lot more personal. I never cease to get goose bumps when I count back the growth rings and find the year of my own birthday."

And here you meet the old Ozark mountaineer who denied being a craftsman because, as his son explained, "his work is part of our way of life, not an art." And which of us dares draw a harsh frontier between craft and art and life?

To any good craftsman, Pygmalion offers a believable story. *Of course*, the sculptor fell in love with his completed statue of Galatea: Don't all of us fall in love with our creations? When a reader enjoys a book that I have helped to shape, I am pleased; but if the same person praises the new kitchen cabinets I have just finished—well, I confess, *that* is a joy I do not have to share with co-workers. After all, "Criticism comes easier than craftsmanship," said Zeuxis of Greece in the fifth century B.C. And who was Zeuxis? A painter—and a fine fellow craftsman.

GILBERT M. GROSVENOR

Folk-art sculpture or plain shingles, vanes have signaled changing weather since the colonists came. An iron snake of unusual design senses the invisible wind. Under a nearly life-size warrior dating from about 1810, letters TO,TE may stand for a secret society. An 1850's mermaid carved in pine grips her comb and mirror. America's most famous weather vane, the glass-eyed copper grasshopper made in 1749 by tinsmith Shem Drowne, still survives Boston's gales above Faneuil Hall.

Contents

Foreword 5
GILBERT M. GROSVENOR

1 Homeland and Handwork 8
C. MALCOLM WATKINS

2 In the American Grain 28
TOM MELHAM

A Nautical Portfolio 66
TOM MELHAM

3 From the American Earth 72
ANDY LEON HARNEY

4 Fiber and Fabric 94
CYNTHIA RUSS RAMSAY

5 In the Mountains 124
CLAY ANDERSON

Toys: A Portfolio of Magic 150
BEVERLY SPOTSWOOD

6 The Scene Today 164
PATRICIA L. RAYMER

Epilogue 194

Authors' Notes 195

Acknowledgments 195

Index 196

1

Homeland and Handwork

THE WORD "CRAFTSMAN" never entered my vocabulary until I grew up. During my boyhood in eastern Massachusetts, after World War I, there were still many people who did things with their hands and did them well. At the time I took them for granted, as I did the newsboy or the iceman. Now I realize that few of them were young.

My grandfather, for instance, could make anything out of wood—or so I believed. Because I was a rail buff at age five, he made me a splendid model of a trolley car, complete with tracks. He was an insurance man, though, and no one in the family would have thought of calling him a craftsman.

Yet, by inheritance and early training, he *was* a craftsman.

His father had been a cabinetmaker for Donald McKay in East Boston, building interior fittings in the elegant clipper ships for which McKay was famous. Great-grandfather even constructed a ship of his own, the square-rigger *Red Cloud*. But he did not build her until 1877, long after oceangoing steamers had made the sailing ship obsolete in all but magnificence. Evidently he was a better craftsman than businessman.

Under his strict scrutiny, my grandfather learned an ancient craft tradition and the uses of hand tools to create things. But the world of the 1870's led him to rely on something else for a living: a white collar and an office and the business of risks and finance. There were many like him.

I spent my boyhood summers in Gloucester. Seafaring and fishing supported the town as they had done for 300 years. Along the waterfront I used to breathe the pungent smells of tar and oakum and fish, and hang around the marine shops where skilled workmen plied their trades.

On the "railways" for repairing vessels out of water I could see painters scraping bottoms, caulkers filling seams, ship's carpenters replacing old or damaged planks. In a sail

ELAINE POWELL

by C. Malcolm Watkins

Unwinding her shuttle, Cecilia Klene demonstrates weaving with the Rose Path pattern, pillowcase width, at northern Virginia's postcolonial Sully Plantation. Household looms like this supplied almost all American families before the Industrial Revolution.

loft where a shopping center stands now, I watched a dozen or so old men, sitting on their long benches, sewing away with their needles and sailmaker's palms—the leather shield that protects the hand.

In Essex, the inland town next to Gloucester, members of a family named Story built wooden fishing vessels and other sailing craft as they had done for generations—certainly since 1813 and possibly earlier. They used tools of the old types to shape ribs and planking by centuries-old techniques. I remember launchings there as great events.

Bright with flags, the sparkling new vessel started down the ways into the Essex River when the owner's wife or pretty daughter cracked a bottle of rum across the bow; the crowd cheered loudly; the ship hit the water with a splash.

Thus the residues of a handcraft society were all around during my boyhood, even though factories were filling our lives with mass-produced goods. In the long perspective of history, after all, only a moment or two had passed since craftsmen made everything used in America.

Until the 1850's the majority of goods remained the work of craftsmen. Before 1800 hand process was virtually the only process. We may treasure a special handmade item—I still have my trolley car!—but we cannot understand the life of the past without a wider view of craftsmanship.

Of all the craftsmen in America's past, none has achieved more splendid success than the Indian. I hold this opinion as an amateur, and as a New Englander I took a long time to reach it.

My parents and grandparents told me of Indians as historical figures, and I heard indignant remarks about the white man's injustice, but I don't recall much attention to Indian craftsmanship. One rare exception was the basket that held Mother's clothespins —of a type peddled from door to door.

Many Americans, I imagine, grew up with similar attitudes.

Then, as a young man, I visited the Museum of the American Indian, Heye Foundation, in New York City, and the richness of Indian artistry fully impressed me.

At first I noticed things that looked familiar. At Old Sturbridge Village in Massachusetts, I had handled some wooden bowls of hand-shaped burl—quite unlike colonial bowls turned on a lathe. Now I saw more of this handwork, and realized that Indian ceremonial bowls had passed into colonial use.

Other wonderful objects opened my eyes further. I recall a redware pottery bowl from Louisiana, an effigy bowl with feline head and writhing, snakelike decorative lines. Even more dramatic was a stone effigy pipe from Spiro Mound in Oklahoma: a warrior beheading a victim.

After that visit, as it happens, I became a museum man myself, at the Smithsonian Institution in Washington, D. C. I have studied American crafts ever since, and though I have specialized in work that comes from the European tradition, I have found Indian crafts equally impressive.

For example, little except painted pottery survives from the prehistoric Mimbres culture of New Mexico. The Smithsonian has numerous pieces, and exhibits a black and white bowl that bears a stylized grasshopper of startling sophistication. When I first saw that pottery, I felt as though I had received a communication from a civilization long forgotten, a spiritual message from a craftsman alive in the sherds of his work.

And a living potter, Helen Cordero of Cochiti Pueblo, conveyed the full intensity of a craftsman's happiness in good work during a conversation we had quite recently. Helen's "storyteller" figures merge her own delightful imagination with ancient folk tradition. Each variation keeps the basic elements: a jolly, rotund narrator sitting on the ground, with wrigglesome or pensive children seated on each leg or cuddled in the bend of an arm or perched on each shoulder to gaze about.

My wife, Joan, had commissioned Helen to make a storyteller figure for the World Crafts Council's exhibition in Toronto in 1974. Helen called me from New Mexico, full of pride in this new piece. "It came out *so beautifully!*" she said. "You have to open the box and see it as soon as it comes!"

Beyond that satisfaction lies the craftsman's knowledge of the things that don't come out so well—as when the clay cracks in firing— and the artist's discontent with a shape that isn't perfect yet.

Thus Helen speaks for the outstanding craftsmen who express their own creativity. Among the most notable of these is Maria Martinez of San Ildefonso Pueblo. She, with her late husband, Julian, raised the black pottery of her tribe to an artistic level that has made her famous.

Home-builders in early America used local materials to advantage. Wilderness pioneers axed down trees for log cabins, working alone or at "raisings" (above). Time permitting, they might square the logs and dovetail the corners. Swedish subjects introduced the log house about 1640. But centuries before the Spanish in New Mexico made clay into sun-dried brick, Indians built adobe houses and patched them much as a woman of Taos does today.

LOWELL GEORGIA WALTER MEAYERS EDWARDS

Helen also speaks for craftsmen known only by surviving work, like the finely woven baskets from California. Or the splendid woodcarving of the Haidas and the Tlingits. Or the silverwork of the Navajos, who adopted this art from an alien white culture and made it distinctively their own.

And pride in accomplishment links the Indian crafts with the rest of the rich history of crafts in America, the traditions the white man brought from Europe.

In the early days of the colonists and the frontier settlements, farm and home were centers of craftsmanship. Craft products met basic needs. One of my favorite examples is on display at the Smithsonian.

This is a 17th-century bedstead that reflects the Puritan austerity of its origins in Essex County, Massachusetts. Its maker lived ten miles from Salem, the nearest town—a long way then. He needed a bedstead, so he made it by the easiest method.

To square its oak posts, he used an adz, a cutting tool as old as the English language, with an inward-curving blade at right angles to the handle. Then he beveled, or chamfered, the posts, just as he would have finished the beams of his house.

One day several years ago I was in the museum, looking at this bed, when a stern-looking lady stopped beside me.

"I have a bed like that, only mine's prettier," she announced.

Unwisely, I volunteered that "this bed was made entirely by hand."

The lady withered me with a glare and rebuked me in ringing tones: "Young man, don't you *know* that *everything* was made by hand in *those* days?" She swept away without waiting for an answer; clearly, she wanted no response from a young upstart. (I was a mere 53 at the time.)

She didn't give me the chance to explain that "handmade" for *those* days involves a matter of degree. I should have called the bedstead "homemade—not shopmade."

If the bedmaker had lived in Salem, he could have gone to the shop of a turner and ordered rounded posts turned on a lathe.

The turner still used his hands skillfully to execute shapes in wood, but he had the help of a machine. He powered it with a foot treadle, or his apprentice turned it by a crank, and as the wood rotated in the lathe the turner applied special tools to cut the decorative profiles called turnings.

Turned posts are indeed prettier, but still made by hand. The lady was right!

Both shop and machine were European in origin, of course, and distinguish colonial from Indian crafts. On the same principle, the colonial potter relied on the potter's wheel to rotate his clay. The housewife energized her spinning wheel to help produce her yarn. The pewterer used molds and lathes to shape and finish his wares.

Such devices saved the craftsman's time and speeded up production. It was only a step beyond, but a revolutionary one, to introduce new sources of power. Water or steam could drive several spinning wheels at once, or a series of lathes, or a group of potter's wheels. The next step brought devices that no longer needed the human hand, such as mechanized spinning wheels.

From the early 19th century onward, in America as in Europe, the need for craftsmanly skill became less as mechanical technology increased. With external power, more and more machines could run in unison. The individual worker had to obey the rhythms of the machines.

And as factories grew, a worker no longer made something from start to finish. Now he did a single task, one of a series, over and over. Less and less could he work for the pride of accomplishment—for the joy of telling a friend that something "came out so beautifully!"

I remember my high-school class visit to an automobile plant, the very symbol of the industrial assembly line. The long moving lines of chassis and auto bodies dominated the men, with each worker timing his movements to the speed of the system. To me as a teenager, it seemed inhuman.

I knew one of the workmen, a French-Canadian who did odd jobs for my grandparents on Saturdays. Once or twice I asked him about the system he worked in; his answers were polite but wary. With children to clothe and feed, he could not afford indiscretions that might get back to the factory. But he could not conceal a cold resentment or convey any enthusiasm for his work there.

Years later I remembered him when I saw Charlie Chaplin's classic movie *Modern Times* and watched its modest hero, "the little fellow," struggle with the relentless assembly line. Underneath the hilarity, the film satirized the dehumanizing effects of the factory. Just recently I saw it again on television.

Chaplin's genius made articulate what I felt when I first saw the line in action. By defining the terrifying opposite of the craftsman, Chaplin implied what the craftsman enjoys: freedom in the use of his skills.

We can recognize extreme cases easily: the craftsman who uses hand tools to make something from start to finish, like the Essex County bedmaker; or the factory worker who tightens a single bolt, hundreds of times a day. Somewhere in the gray areas between, the craftsman becomes a semiskilled employee.

I suspect this point comes when the worker no longer directs the machine to do what *he* wants, in a personal creative choice. And when he can't turn the machine off at will, as the turner in Salem could have stopped his lathe to enjoy a mug of cider.

In colonial times, the term craftsman covered many different kinds of people, also referred to as artisan, tradesman, and artificer. I've never found much consistency in these labels, even in their own day.

"Artisan" might apply to a master goldsmith, someone as respected as Paul Revere. But often it was interchangeable with "tradesman," and that fits anyone who works at a trade: potter, printer, broom-maker, blacksmith, baker, butcher, tanner, or candlestick-maker. "Artificer" was apparently a fancier term for a person with an unusual skill. It might refer to someone who made scientific instruments, or to a brass founder—as Revere, in later years, became.

Skill imposes its own distinctions, and the order of professional craftsmen has always been a hierarchy. In colonial times, the master craftsman stood at the top. Usually he ran his own shop, set the standards, determined the designs, and directed his subordinates. Sometimes he might accept the designs of a talented customer, as an architect today would use the sketches of a client who knows just what he wants.

If he served the wealthy—as silversmiths and cabinetmakers did—he pleased his customer by following fashions set in Europe, not by introducing radical new patterns of his own. The richer the client, the more likely he was to hold the craftsman to the established order. There were exceptions, notably Thomas Jefferson; but most rich customers had conservative tastes, and made them stick.

Thus the master craftsman worked within definite limits, beyond those imposed by the wood or the silver itself. Yet he enjoyed definite freedom—literal copying from European models or pattern books was rare. He gave his work its own quality.

Paul Revere, an outstanding master, developed a clearly individual manner. A connoisseur of American silver can usually spot a Revere piece before he looks at the maker's mark. I once saw the late John Marshall Phillips, of the Yale University Art Gallery, zero in without hesitation on an innocent-looking tankard with Revere's mark. "That finial's wrong! Revere would never have made a lid like that!" he said with finality.

We can all be sure that not every genuine marked piece represents only the work of Revere—or any comparable silversmith. In his shop, as in a master cabinetmaker's, journeymen did much of the work. Yet the master supervised it, and I think we have evidence of what this meant to Revere himself.

Then, as now, someone sitting for a portrait usually wore formal clothes for the occasion. But Revere posed for John Singleton Copley in his shirtsleeves, holding a teapot and displaying the tools of his trade. In his own eyes he was the master craftsman, who still worked on the things that bore his name; he had the ultimate responsibility, whatever his journeymen contributed.

The journeyman had established his skill by completing an apprenticeship. He might settle down in one shop with the possibility of becoming master someday. He might prefer to remain an employee all his life.

I once knew a journeyman potter, who moved from shop to shop in North Carolina. He made whatever the shop specialized in, whether teacups or strawberry planters, with flawless skill. At the end of the day he went home to his family, leaving the master potter to worry about meeting the customers or keeping the kiln fired or paying the bills.

In colonial times, the master usually agreed to teach his apprentice something beyond the craft: reading, writing, calculating weights and measures, keeping accounts.

The apprentice would serve about seven years, doing the dirty work, learning his skill by constant repetition. He promised to obey all his master's "lawfull Commands gladly," as one indenture put it, never to "frequent Taverns" or play cards or dice, and not to marry. When his term ended, the master would give him a "freedom suit"—new clothes for a new life.

I've always been especially fond of one of

the least spectacular exhibits we have at the Smithsonian: a freedom suit in natural linen, of buttoned jacket and knee breeches. It belonged to Jonathan Sheldon, apprentice to a noted cabinetmaker in Newport—a slender boy, obviously, only five feet tall. Plain and durable, honestly earned and carefully preserved, that suit tells me more about the life of the 18th century than the lace and satins that descendants prefer to keep. In Jonathan's time, after all, Americans decided to favor freedom over elegance!

From the years of the Revolution, but from a different tradition, come two more imposing objects: wooden sculptures representing St. Gabriel and St. Michael. Once these *santos*—saints—stood near the altar of the mission church at the Zuni pueblo in New Mexico. In 1880 an early ethnologist salvaged them from the mission ruins for the Smithsonian. Skillfully carved, bright with paint and gold leaf from Spain, these two santos would not have been out of place in an 18th-century church in Europe.

A friend and colleague, known by her own wish simply as E. Boyd, identified them as the work of a Spanish settler named Bernardo Miera y Pacheco. He lived in Santa Fe from about 1754 until his death in 1785. E. Boyd found that he was not a reclusive little woodcarver working alone in a shed but a painter in oils, an explorer, the outstanding mapmaker of colonial New Mexico, a soldier with the then-important rank of captain.

Cartographer, sculptor, and glorifier of God, Miera y Pacheco establishes the dignity of crafts on the colonial Spanish frontier and the lingering ideal of the Renaissance man, not only brave but versatile.

His successors in the 19th century no longer enjoyed a direct connection with the cosmopolitan culture of Mexico City. These *santeros*, or saint-makers, were folk-craftsmen; they made less sophisticated but often more powerful figures, objects of popular devotion. Their tradition thrives today, though the collector is now the principal patron.

Contemporary santeros carve stylized figures as a rule, and leave the wood unpainted and ungilded; they include details from the life around them.

My wife has acquired several of these modern works. The first was a carving of *El Santo Niño*—the Holy Child. He appears as a seated boy wearing a flat-brimmed hat, holding a basket in one hand and a shepherd's crook

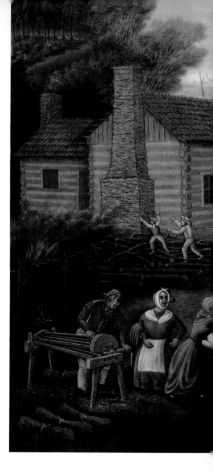

Mixing pleasure with the drudgery of processing flax, neighbors in Pennsylvania meet at a "scutching bee" in the 1850's. A wooden "brake" at far left crushes the flax stalks. Then hard pounding with paddlelike wooden scutching knives separates the crushed core and woody sheathing from fibers used for linen thread. Flax seeds provided linseed oil, a standard preservative for wooden items. Here a staff man oils an elm-wood ox yoke at the re-created town of Old Sturbridge Village, Massachusetts. Though the farmer oiled—and often carved—his own yoke, he usually took his metalwork to a blacksmith or to a farrier, specialist in horseshoeing.

NATIONAL GEOGRAPHIC PHOTOGRAPHER BATES LITTLEHALES

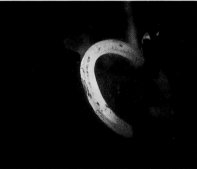

LOWELL GEORGIA

15

Restored to 17th-century dignity, New England's Seth Story house blends varied furnishings around a hearth for cold winters. With large chimney and small entryway, this room—a display at the Henry Francis du Pont Winterthur Museum in Delaware—once comprised the entire ground floor. The four-armed click reel measured yarn. A "court cupboard" dated 1684 held cherished possessions; style and workmanship suggest the hand of Thomas Dennis, perhaps America's first furniture-maker of note. Its lathe-turned corner posts contrast with the adz-cut bed in the house's upper room, reassembled at the Smithsonian Institution. Such furniture reflects an age when nearly every homeowner was a jack-of-all-trades— and master of some. But as America grew, cabinetmakers from Europe began setting up shop in the flourishing towns, and the specialist increasingly supplanted the home craftsman.

in the other. Its maker was the first santero I met: José Mondragón, whose dignified manner suggests the pride of Spain.

In a little shop in the mountain village of Chimayo, he carves the saints and Biblical subjects he heard of as a child; and his wife, Alice—who carves small animals—helps with details like the final sanding.

"The saints and holy figures are very real to these carvers," Joan believes, "the Santo Niño especially—the *santuario* at Chimayo is dedicated to Him." People from miles around go there for miraculous cures.

In the same town lives an older santero, Apolonio Martinez. Joan and I visited him—and shared his wife's delicious tortillas—when he had just completed his wonderful rendering of the expulsion from Eden. On a white-pine plank 27 inches long, he grouped five carvings in aspen wood. Red cedar emphasizes the fateful apples on the tree at right. A crowned angel stands behind Adam and Eve, who stride toward the seated figure of *La Muerte*—Death, holding a sickle.

In Martinez' own charming translation from Spanish, he has labeled this work "The Tree of the Science of Good and Bad," and he has carefully written out his explanations of each detail. As holds true for authentic folk craftsmen, he works with themes and emotions that run deep in his culture.

Of all the crafts, those of building a house seem to me the most expressive. And to me, a classic example is the timber-framed house of Seth Story, of the same family as the Essex shipbuilders of my childhood days.

He built it about 1690; and we can safely assume that he followed ancient craft precepts, for the county records list him as "house Carpenter" and "Housewright."

Story cut down oak trees with his felling ax, and chopped them up on the spot for posts and beams. He squared and trimmed them to remarkable smoothness with his broadax. Then he cut slots and tongues, called mortises and tenons, for joints. Fitting the joints together, he bored holes through them. Later he could secure them with wooden pegs, or "tree-nails." New Englanders still pronounce this as he did—and spell it—"trunnels."

With a few helpers, Story hauled his finished timbers to the site where he had prepared a cellar and a stone foundation. The men laid out the pieces on the ground, fitted them together, pounded in the trunnels.

And then came the house-raising. Neighbors gathered to help—or watch. Men lifted each section of wall to a manageable angle by hand; they shoved it vertical with poles until the corners came together. One of the more agile carpenters scrambled up the frame to secure the joints with more trunnels. Soon they had the frame intact, the roof in place.

Usually, on these occasions, everyone enjoyed good food and a liberal flow of spirits. A new home deserved a celebration, and willing neighbors earned a reward.

More than a century after Seth Story completed his house, a well-to-do man named Eben Parsons observed the raising of his new mansion at Byfield, Massachusetts. An eyewitness, Sarah Anna Emery, told how crowds assembled by carriage, horseback, and foot.

"Deft hands splendidly did the work . . . the master builder, Mr. Stephen Tappan of Newburyport, appeared on the summit, bottle in hand. . . . with a cheer which was caught up . . . by the multitude, the new roof-tree was duly baptized in pure old Jamaica."

Now the guests arranged themselves on a platform built over the floor beams, the minister held forth for nearly an hour, and a mixed chorus sang to the accompaniment of a bass viol.

Foolproof craftsmanship has never been a certainty—the platform then crashed into the cellar, honored guests and all!

Evidently nobody was injured; a "sumptuous entertainment was served," and wrestling contests and races went on until dark.

Although later innovations doomed the mortise-and-tenon timber frame, that sturdy technique survived until well past 1850. Even today, Amish farmers build their barns this way, with community raisings for each.

Pioneers took this technique westward, all the way to California. I first became aware of this when a timber-frame house almost interrupted my honeymoon.

With Joan at my side, I was driving south from San Francisco on the coast highway. We were passing the outskirts of Half Moon Bay, when a glance up a sloping hillside challenged my credulity: a weathered gray colonial-New-England-style "saltbox" house. Ghostlike and windowless, this was as startling in California as a dinosaur would be.

Abruptly, I turned up the lane—some sharp queries in my ears—only to find the house surrounded by impassable plots of Brussels sprouts and irrigation sprinklers.

Later Joan and I returned for a detailed

study. We found that the house had a frame of mortise-and-tenoned redwood, and its prefabricated timbers bore the Roman numerals that joiners had used for centuries as codes for assembling a framework. Thus we could show that a craft tradition from medieval Europe had crossed an ocean and a continent.

Home interiors, of course, reflect changes of fashion and taste more quickly than structural methods do. That California house had a Victorian decor, with ornament foreign to a Puritan home like Seth Story's. We might prefer his—in the 17th century, structure was integral with design.

Story covered the interior board walls with plaster made of clay, lime from crushed seashells, marsh grass, and red cow's hair. He left naked the beams and corner posts and ceilings. Finally, he mounted hinged casement windows, with latticed strips of lead that held tiny diamond-shaped panes of glass.

Loving craftsmanship, distilled through centuries of tradition, proved its creativity in the result: an effect of dignity, handsome proportions, harmony with the landscape. Inside, dark woodwork contrasted with whitewashed plaster. Warm-brown wide boards set off the brick fireplaces. Sunlight cast a crosshatch of diamond shadows on the walls and floor in delightful patterns.

I doubt if Seth Story was aware of all these subtleties. But consciously or not, applying his time-honored skills, he made the just and correct judgments that result in architecture of genuine distinction. Thus he exemplifies the craftsmen who contributed in such variety to America's manmade environment.

And out of his craftsmanship we learn something about him that we otherwise could not know. Seth Story was essentially anonymous. His name appears on a few deeds and other records. Otherwise, he died unsung.

He was not a man of regional fame, like Governor John Winthrop, or national fame, like George Washington or Thomas Jefferson. Men like these become living figures to us in portraits and unending documents. Their homes simply provide added details.

With a man like Seth Story, however, our only significant form of communication with him is the house he built. It tells us how sound a craftsman he was, how carefully he provided for his family, what his culture derived from. By evidence like this we learn about the ordinary people of history.

We can easily lose it, unfortunately. When I

With fire and anvil, the blacksmith forged the ironwork essential to any settlement. He made many everyday necessities such as handwrought nails; he repaired the tools of shop and farm and hearth, including gridirons and shovels. Sometimes, especially on the frontier, his ambition exceeded his capability—as in one 18th-century Virginian's scroll hinge, clumsily imitating the German-made hinge beneath it.

Overleaf: Community effort and sturdy mortise-and-tenon construction, both widespread in America three centuries ago, still mark barn-raisings in Amish country. Precut timbers speed up the work; scurrying boys fetch tools and pegs. Women cook for the occasion, quilt or chat with neighbors while frame and roof and walls reach completion within a day.

first knew the Story house, enlargements and "improvements" had disguised it, and about 1957 it seemed doomed to demolition. The great collector Henry Francis du Pont learned about it, acquired it, and saved it.

Through the Henry Francis du Pont Winterthur Museum, he had it dismantled with scientific care and re-erected the original first-floor room as an exhibit. I arranged for the Smithsonian to acquire the second-floor room, now on display in the National Museum of History and Technology. Both rooms bear witness to traditional American craftsmanship and the housebuilder's art.

Of course there were other notable types of both. The log house became a national symbol; an Anglo-Irish traveler in 1795 concluded that "These habitations are not very sightly, but when well built they are warm and comfortable and last a long time."

In the arid lands of the Southwest, the Spanish colonizers built their houses and churches of sun-dried brick—*adobes* of clay and straw—and created extraordinary sculptured architecture. Missions and towns and ranches reveal the craftsman's resourcefulness in a land lacking many raw materials.

Once I walked through a New Mexico mountain village with a proper Bostonian lady. A scholarly person for whom I have great respect, she was on unfamiliar ground on her first visit to the backcountry of the Southwest. It was fall; and the adobe houses around the village plaza bore strings of vivid scarlet chili peppers, drying against the white façades. My friend stopped, wide-eyed. In the clear accents of the Back Bay, she exclaimed, "Oh, beautiful, red lobsters!"

Comprehending the regional diversity of American ways is difficult enough in our own day, and challenges our appreciation of crafts in their native setting. Distance in time can mislead us further. We can easily recognize the beauty of colonial textiles and miss the rigors of an age when just keeping warm in winter must have been a constant preoccupation. In New England in the 17th century or the Appalachians in the early 20th, making warm clothing and blankets or quilts was as essential as providing shelter.

Except for the wealthy, domestic textile crafts were all but universal. In 1769 alone, Middleton, Massachusetts—population 500—turned out 20,522 yards of cloth, entirely the work of family craftsmen.

Sarah Anna Emery remembered her girlhood of about 1800, when she made daily visits to an aunt and uncle at Newbury, Massachusetts. Her uncle cultivated one of the best orchards in the neighborhood, and raised sheep and swine; he was also a professional weaver. "After a hard day's work out of doors," Mrs. Emery wrote, "it was no infrequent thing to hear his loom till twelve or one o'clock at night."

Sarah's uncle exemplifies a balance between agriculture and domestic craftsmanship characteristic of rural Americans. And this balance helped account for the flexibility we often call Yankee ingenuity.

The need to make things on the farm kept sharp the edge of this ingenuity, and often led to the fabrication of machines. Mrs. Emery described a number of inventive craftsmen in her own neighborhood.

One was Jacob Perkins, who began his career in Newburyport as a goldsmith. After devising a method for silver-plating shoe buckles, he closed his business in 1787 to develop a machine for cutting and heading nails in a single rapid operation.

This eliminated two aspects of craftwork: the blacksmith's forging of nails by hand, one at a time, hammer stroke by hammer stroke; and the carpenter's boring holes in boards, one at a time, before driving a hand-forged nail. The saving in time and money is obvious —an official report in 1810 reckoned it as high as "twenty *per cent.* of the value of the article."

Such innovations fostered America's version of the industrial revolution. The New World had undone the first shackles of tradition and hierarchical society. The new nation, with a heady spirit of freedom and equality, unfastened the rest. The very qualities that had brought the craft system to its highest levels now prepared the craftsman to turn away from old habits. Directing his skills to inventive zeal, as Perkins did, the craftsman began the destruction of the system that made his skills possible.

Towns and cities played their part as well. From the beginning they had fostered a steadily increasing sophistication and specialization in the crafts.

One shipment of Irish indentured servants "to be disposed of" in Boston in 1716 illustrates this. The men consisted of "Anchor & Ship Smith, House Carpenters, Ship Joyners and Carver, Cooper, Shoemakers, and Pattoun Maker, Naylors, Lock-Smiths, Currier, Taylor, Book Printer, Silver-Gold Lace Weaver, Silver Smith." The women included "Milliners, Ribband & Lace Weavers, Button Maker, Earthen Ware Potter Maker."

Women potters were unusual in the 18th century; and the experience of one shows how hard it can be to assess the role of women in crafts. Grace Parker of Charlestown, Massachusetts, was a potter of the 1740's who inherited the management of an enterprise after her husband died. But she had to take her brother-in-law as a partner to have a man as titular head of the firm. No one can say how many other businesses concealed active women behind masculine names.

Yet women held certain crafts and occupations as their own, such as ribbon-weaving. They shared with men the demanding craft of wax working, which included portraiture. And their household experience may well have influenced the development of American furniture, even if indirectly.

One of the most splendid and successful crafts of the pre-industrial era, cabinetmaking reveals quite dramatically the Americanization of a European model. The massive "joined" oak furniture of the 1600's reflects the English past: all that was solid, respectable—and hard to move.

Much more typical and characteristically American was simpler furniture, quickly made, like six-board pine chests, nailed together rather than joined, or plain ladderback chairs. A good example, now in the Smithsonian collection, is the "great chair" that Jonathan Copp of Stonington, Connecticut, mentioned in a will dated 1746. In its restrained turnings it follows the style of its time, but in lightness of construction it looks ahead to the goal of getting more out of less.

This aspiration emerged repeatedly in the work of American craftsmen. Time and money were usually at a premium in pioneer country; craftwork shows it in subdued ornament, functional efficiency, and strong, clean lines.

In a house like Seth Story's, with only two rooms, people needed movable furniture, easily adjusted to the changing uses of the room in the course of a day. Craftsmen devised folding bedsteads, and tilt-top tables convertible into seats.

And pioneers were often people who moved on. The lighter the furniture, the more easily carried along. Very early in our history, craftsmen applied their ingenuity to practical things for American modes of life.

"You get good results this way," comments my friend Sam Maloof, who assesses furniture in the light of his own mastery of the craft. "It's best when you work out your own design in the wood, for an individual purchaser, and think of its use in everyday living." American craftsmen weren't "trying for difference for its own sake," in his words, but for practical and handsome things—and difference followed naturally.

Probably the most striking example in 18th-century furniture is the American Windsor chair. The colonial chairmaker scrapped the English prototype and made a tough, durable, light structure. In all its variations it emphasizes a minimum of wood and the strength that comes from balance and tension in design. Like the wheels of a racing gig, it is mobile, light, and strong.

Other instances of Americanization occur. At Newport, Rhode Island, cabinetmakers of the Goddard and Townsend families developed their "block-front" chests, desks, and secretaries with shell-motif ornament as a dramatic and original New England style.

Members of a genuine folk culture, the Pennsylvania Germans kept their favorite motifs—birds, tulips and other flowers—and worked them into hardware, slip-decorated pottery, textiles, and painted furniture.

Yet with the great events of the Revolution, their potters altered some motifs. They took a German folk figure, the Horseman of the Apocalypse riding a white horse, and turned him into a Continental cavalryman—or George Washington himself. And the Biblical eagle of Revelation became an American one.

And sometimes the frontier craftsman attempted work quite beyond his skill. A blacksmith tried to make a scroll hinge, of a type familiar in Germany, for one Jost Hite's house in western Virginia in the mid-18th century. But the elaborate curves were too much for him; he plainly bit off more than he could chew!

The most skillful craftsman might fail in business, as several early glassworkers did. Johann Friedrich Amelung arrived in Baltimore in 1784 with 68 trained workmen he had spirited out of Germany. He settled near Sugar Loaf Mountain in central Maryland, in a beautiful New World wilderness. He built a factory, houses for his employees and a brick mansion for himself, and schools. Soon he was producing bottles and window glass, but he had a hard struggle with unfamiliar local ingredients to make good clear table glass.

He succeeded in this, but he never found customers enough; he kept expanding his plant, his staff, and his debts. In 1795 he went bankrupt; soon after, he died.

Amelung had produced superb engraved presentation items, and I once had the Federal Bureau of Investigation compare his signature with engraved examples of his name. Its experts were noncommittal—the glass may or may not have been engraved by "the subject." But a windowpane from his mansion, preserved as a relic in Frederick, bears an inscription he scratched with a diamond: "Thinking sad thoughts." And the date May 7, 1790—the day after his first factory had burned down.

Although Amelung's ambition outran his means, his skilled craftsmen helped establish a successful glass industry in America.

In the special conditions of the South, crafts remained to a large extent in the hands of indentured white servants and black slaves. Many planters saw the value of training Negroes, to avoid the expense of paying free craftsmen or to gain extra income by hiring out their slave specialists.

Advertisements for runaway slaves suggest the number of craftsmen among them. For example, William Digges, Jr., published a notice in the *Maryland Gazette* of February 27, 1755, for his "dark Mulatto Man, named *Sam* . . . a Carpenter. . . . HE IS AN ARTFUL FELLOW AND CAN READ AND WRITE. . . ." And according to an 1803 notice from Charleston, South Carolina, one John had worked as a "journeyman with a Windsor Chairmaker" and was "well acquainted with the use of the joiners tools."

Numerous black potters worked in South Carolina. One was Dave, of Aiken County; a jar in the Charleston Museum bears the date "31st July 1840" and the inscription: "Dave belongs to Mr. Miles / Where the oven bakes / & the pot biles."

"Free persons of color"—as the law called them—who were craftsmen may have fared better than others in a society with ambivalent feelings about them. A noteworthy example was Thomas Day of Milton, in Caswell County, North Carolina.

Supposedly he came from the West Indies. Demonstrably he was a skilled cabinetmaker. From the 1830's through the 1850's he made mahogany and rosewood furniture for leading families of the area. Considering the racial taboos of those days, Tom Day's white neighbors accorded him a singular respect.

One still-remembered incident sheds light on his situation and his times: When he made a set of handsome mahogany pews for Milton's Presbyterian Church, he did so only with the understanding that he should always have the privilege of sitting in one of them with his family during church services.

As the 19th century wore on, many craftsmen survived in rural areas and in traditional services, such as ship-caulking in old towns like Gloucester. Some followed the pioneers westward. But more and more surrendered to a fast-expanding factory system. In the process the workman—no longer a craftsman—lost his old independence and self-direction.

To be sure, mass production of cheap consumer goods let poor people own more things; in many ways it improved their lives. But often it destroyed standards of craftsmanship and vulgarized popular taste. At Philadelphia's great Centennial Exposition in 1876, people gazed with awe at the new machines—and the things they turned out: cast-iron gewgaws, ornate furniture, fancy silver-plated ware, stiflingly lavish fabrics.

Inevitably a reaction followed, and it began at the top. Well-to-do, educated men and women adopted the objectives of the English arts and crafts movement and led an American counterpart. Maria Longworth Nichols Storer brought together amateur and professional ceramists at her Rookwood Pottery in Cincinnati. Louis Comfort Tiffany of New York, as a decorator and designer, orchestrated the work of glassblowers and other craftsmen under his strong direction.

In this essentially upper-class movement, craftsmen worked self-consciously as artists. Their ethic is expressed by a living craftsman, ship carver Willard Shepard of Mystic Seaport in Connecticut: "It is better to make one thing right than a million things wrong."

Such craftsmen have many successors today, some young and some not, who see the crafts as a sane balance to life in a commercially oriented world. My wife and I have friends among them: Hal Painter for one, who produces tapestries of great beauty and lives in a log cabin in the forests of Oregon, where his loom is the most important object about him.

Many students and some Ph.D.'s have turned their backs on conventional occupations to become craftsmen. In Sam Maloof's words, they are searching for "something that began with the beginning of civilization—working with their hands!" At such a routine trade as carpentry, young men are reviving an honorable craft that has suffered from a lowering of standards.

I have met one, only 24 years old, who specializes in historic preservation. He feels that the skills of colonial carpenters have a special meaning for him; in restoring their work he learns their methods and reasons for following them.

"I want to master a process," he says. "I want to complete something, to make my own decisions." He tries to avoid routine jobs and hack work, to sidestep the competitiveness of the business world.

I sympathize, for at his age I avoided my father's insurance business in favor of a museum career and its special challenge: preserving craftwork as part of our heritage.

And Joan, out of long experience as artist-craftsman and teacher, has an emphatic explanation: "These young people are reaching for something more human, more natural. They are finding satisfaction in making things from beginning to end. In this way they are preserving their independence."

Those who turn to the crafts, I think, are not trying to turn the clock back. They are trying to find themselves, in fundamental relationships between hand and material, between man and nature.

Such relationships have taken distinctive forms in America, and I have had the good fortune to see them through the eyes of a museum man. The Story house and the *Red Cloud*, Helen Cordero's storytellers, José Mondragón's saints and Tom Day's church pews—all these express the human capacity to be creative. I suspect that anyone who admires American craftwork has examples just as valid; no single collection, no one book, could begin to hold them. And I suspect that anyone who tries craftwork knows its goal: to shape in lasting and meaningful ways the world in which we have lived.

In America's early glassworks, gaffers from Europe relied on the blowpipe and other hand tools to make bottles and windowpanes. The factories of Caspar Wistar in New Jersey and Henry William Stiegel in Pennsylvania also enjoyed commercial success with luxury wares before the Revolution. Enameled "Stiegel-type" glass and swan-topped sugar bowls reflect old German designs (above). Breaking with tradition in the 1880's and after, Louis C. Tiffany experimented with daringly freeform stained glass in panels (below) and in lamps.

N.G.S. PHOTOGRAPHER BATES LITTLEHALES

DAVID DOUBILET

Surrounded by emblems of maritime history, Willard Shepard carves an 18-inch-high copy of a figurehead from a ship named for singer Jenny Lind, working in the shop at Mystic Seaport in Connecticut. One of the nation's few full-time ship carvers, he sculpts quarter boards and other nautical decorations similar to those of the past century. In the waning era of sail, John Anderson's portrait of Civil War hero David Farragut (far left) marked the bow of the clipper Great Admiral; Creole, a New Orleans packet, also bore a figure appropriate to her name (left). Both escaped the fate that inspired a 19th-century naval officer to lament: "And there's many a story that could be told / Of the fine figureheads that were chiselled of old / On the dreary sands they crumble today / From Terra del Fuego to Baffins Bay."

27

2

In the American Grain

A TALE I'm fond of credits Mark Twain with a peculiar flair for whittling. It seems that one day the snowy-headed Missourian settled himself on his front porch and began carving a hunk of wood with furious abandon. First one passerby, then another and another stopped to watch the old man at work. Lost in his own intense concentration, Twain ignored his impromptu audience, even when people began to speculate on what he was whittling.

Was it a statuette? Walking stick? Whirligig? An argument developed; a couple of men placed a bet on the outcome. Finally curiosity overcame one bystander's shyness: "Excuse me, but what are you making?"

"A pile of shavings," Twain crustily replied.

Talented whittler or not, Mark Twain or not, whoever invented that reply knew something about the rewards of working with wood. Whittling—even if it ends in a 'pile of shavings'—can ease man's tensions and soothe his soul. On top of that, a good whittler can make almost anything, for wood remains the most versatile and probably the most useful of craft materials.

Historically, wood fostered America's rapid growth. Awesome virgin forests—where wild cherry trees grew four or five feet thick— seemed inexhaustible to the settlers. With this resource, they bridged the untamed rivers, shaped the ships, wagons, and barrels of commerce, fashioned tools for agriculture and industry, carved the gears of progress. Toys and fiddles, gunstocks and candlestands, peg legs and weathercocks—all came from wood.

Wood also housed America, and furnished her homes with everything from crude but functional trenchers to Duncan Phyfe chairs. The Goddard family of Newport and other early American masters brought to wood the formal intricacies of shell carvings, flame finials, and ball-and-claw feet; 19th-century Shakers preferred the unadorned simplicity of trestle tables and ladderback chairs. In each generation, cabinetmakers left their own stylistic thumbprint firmly on the wood they worked. Then as now, wood was their perfect medium, a substance not only abundant but beautiful and easily worked. Better yet, it was *warm*.

Something there is in well-worked wood that lures both hand and eye; a vitality, a magnetism, a warmth that aligns with man's very soul. Wood is enduring and ancient. It is also organic, a substance once alive.

"There's a spirit in wood that draws man to touch, feel, be at one with wood," says George Nakashima, one of America's most sought-after contemporary cabinetmakers. Serene at an age he dismisses as irrelevant, this native-born American regards wood with a respect as oriental as his ancestry. He believes in "a partnership between man and wood—neither was meant to live alone." To Nakashima, this partnership demands a reverence, a reverence that encompasses the living tree.

With the zeal of a knight in quest of the Grail, Nakashima scours the globe for trees with "character"—walnut trunks that branch distinctively, or English burl oak that yields a wood of convoluted grain, a wood he calls "alive with fire, joy, and play." These and other unique items eventually reach Nakashima's workshop in wooded Bucks County, Pennsylvania, where the master craftsman strives "to fulfill each tree's destiny, to give it a second life."

Unlike the sawyer who squares a log before ripping it into planks, Nakashima sections each tree "as is." Where edges don't have to be square, they aren't. Instead, they keep the tree's own contour. The resulting free-form designs give each finished piece a dynamism and closeness to nature that have become Nakashima trademarks. But deciding how to slice the trunk can be tricky.

"You're never completely sure what you'll find inside. It's like cutting a diamond—cut one way and you get something beautiful, cut another way and you lose it all."

BY TOM MELHAM

Skilled hands of Ozark mountaineer Harold Enlow whittle a hillbilly statuette from basswood, prized for its detail-holding texture. Whittling—once an all-American pastime—now survives mainly in rural areas, among such self-taught masters of the jackknife. As in the past, wood's workability, abundance, and cradle-to-coffin versatility make it the favorite medium of many American craftsmen today.

Nakashima's clients choose from the cut slabs and indicate what sort of furniture they want. Discussions follow, not only with the clients but with the wood as well.

"I have a kind of dialogue with those slabs," says Nakashima, pointing to weighty panels arrayed about his studio. "Sometimes it takes years—maybe five or more—before I decide what to do with them. You see, there's a tremendous yearning in the wood to fulfill itself. If I don't satisfy that yearning, the wood feels frustrated."

Faultless craftsmanship and modern technology help him make his furniture frustration-free. His shop hums with giant sanders and sophisticated power tools. "Many times, machines do a better job than hand tools. But you have to know how to use them."

Nakashima and his nine assistants know how. In a shop where tolerances approach "a few thousandths of an inch," his men appear as intent as surgeons in the operating room. Gauze masks, worn to keep sawdust out of their noses, intensify that image.

Their precision blossoms in a visual symphony of design and workmanship. A Nakashima pedestal table clasps its gleaming top of buckeye burl as gracefully as a Tiffany setting holds a gem. Its surface polished to silken smoothness, its grain alive with thousands of eddies and whorls of contrasting lines—this table is as much a monument to human skill and empathy for wood as it is an attractive and functional piece of furniture. It is a testament to Nakashima's decades-old "partnership" with wood.

Just down the road from Nakashima live furniture-makers of a totally different sort. Bob Hoffa and Harry Woodward labor with hand tools, not precision machinery. In their early twenties, both lack their renowned neighbor's decades of experience and his worldwide resources. But they don't lack resourcefulness. Unable to afford Nakashima's exotic trees, they seek their wood in Pennsylvania's abandoned barns. Self-taught and inventive, these self-proclaimed rustic craftsmen recycle such aged planking into solid and warm "country furniture." They much prefer old barn wood—stripped of its weathered gray coat—to new lumber.

Harry explained why with two finished pieces of white pine. One was sterile and pasty. "This one's new wood. And this one"—he held up a tawny slat the color of brown sugar—"has about 125 years on it. You can't dupli-cate that patina with stains or anything else."

"The old stuff sure has character," Bob agreed, pointing out a few nicks and other minor flaws bestowed by time. Instead of erasing all such imperfections, Bob and Harry leave some in.

Such natural blemishes lend the work a certain honesty. All is visible, as in spartan Shaker furniture. You can see the wood's grain, tortured or mellow. You can see its age. You can see the straightforward design and solid joints, all painstakingly handmade.

"Furniture *has* to be handcrafted," Harry believes. "It has to have a feeling, a hand-to-wood closeness." Hand planes, not power jointers, pare rough barn planking down to tabletop smoothness. Chisels cut mortises and butterfly joints. Hinges and drawer pulls take shape in a potbellied stove "forge." There's no mystery to this furniture, just simplicity, earnest craftmanship, and a respect for wood.

Linseed oil and beeswax, hand-rubbed into the grain, leave the finished piece looking no more like a barn than gleaming Chippendale chairs resemble their bark-encrusted origins. Asking Bob and Harry to make a table is like having an antique made to order—the wood is old, their method older. The furniture just hasn't been together as long as the wood in a registered antique. But there's no reason it can't last as long. Well-crafted wooden furniture endures, because wood endures.

Endurance—in both design and function—measures the skill of today's craftsmen as it did in America's past. Those who failed to engineer durability into their creations faced ridicule and loss of work, and possibly remorse.

A broken wagon wheel would cause inconvenience, to say the least; a carriage wheel breaking at a gallop might cripple or kill some unlucky passenger. Wheelwrights chose their woods with special care. Some liked gum for the hubs; others preferred white oak or hickory, the woods of choice for spokes and fellies—the outer rims. Two years' seasoning was a minimum for wood that would take the jolts and strains of swamp roads and hill tracks, rocks and frozen ruts and stumps.

Shipwrights felt a heavier responsibility, for their work—from grand paddle-wheeler to dory, frigate to sleek clipper ship—had to stand up to the united wrath of sea and weather. Even after the emergence of iron, shipwrights continued to rely on wood for resilience, workability, and natural endurance.

Of all commercial ships, none took more punishment than the hardy whalers that defied gales in the North Atlantic and hurricanes in the tropics, icebergs, coral reefs, and murderous straits as they sought their mighty quarry from Cape Horn to the frigid Sea of Okhotsk. Survival demanded that whalers be sturdy vessels, ships like the *Charles W. Morgan.*

Launched in 1841 at whaling's zenith, the *Morgan* logged more sea miles than any other American whaler, and outlived them all. Today she lies permanently moored at Mystic Seaport, Connecticut, a re-created shipbuilding community on the Mystic River. Preserved as a national historic landmark, the *Morgan* gleams as if new. All her rigging—including masts, yards, and other spars—has been restored to mint condition.

Her gold-trimmed, shiny black hull still has much of the original wood, wood that survived 80 perilous years of whaling followed by decades of disuse, fire, and storm. Visible from the hull's interior, these pitch-blackened timbers appear charred and cracked. But they remain sound.

Wood that *has* rotted is replaced by master shipwright Henry B. Jarvis, a lean old salt whose eyes crinkle up into slits and whose jaw juts out under a corncob pipe just like a well-known cartoon character's. No wonder his children call him Popeye.

I met Henry in the dark bowels of the *Morgan*'s fo'c'sle, hemmed in by giant timbers, bulkheads, and recently laid "ceiling"—the inner sheathing of the hull. The smell of wood and sea lay thick about; a wood-burning stove topped with bubbling coffeepot gave Henry's cramped quarters a friendly, clam-shack atmosphere.

"To build a ship, you've got to know what woods go where," Henry began, listing examples of nautical know-how. Pine provides ceiling amidships but green oak serves fore and aft, where curves demand a wood that can bend. Instead of nails, trunnels—inch-thick, foot-long pegs of black locust—bond the ship's sheathing to its ribs.

"Black locust, see, is tough and close-grained. It won't break or rot, and it doesn't shrink much. Some places, you might use copper spikes. But wood on wood is best."

Henry's big problem lies in finding his materials. No lumberyard of today stocks massive ships' timbers. And so, with the *Morgan*'s future in mind, Mystic Seaport stockpiles wood that might be needed decades

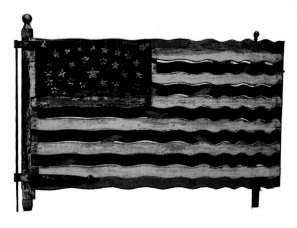

A New York patriot's 36-star flag snaps in an imaginary breeze, and a distinctive gate from Connecticut unites scaled-down farm implements with a still-life carving of harvest bounty. Both depart in style from the split-rail fencing that once enclosed farms of eastern America; both commanded admiration in a 1974 exhibit of folk art, shown here at the Whitney Museum of American Art in New York City.

DAVID DOUBILET

from now. Materials for spars, beams, and planking lie in a protective shed among a hundred or so larch roots.

Larch roots? Right—larch trees, you see, usually put forth one main root. Sometimes that root strikes hardpan clay that deflects it. Then it grows at just the angle and proportions that make it perfect for use as a ship's "knee," one of many big right-angle braces that support the decks. With a couple of able helpers, Henry has replaced a number of *Morgan*'s knees.

"You might have to look through a dozen trees before findin' one with that angle. But it's always better to get wood shaped the way you need it than to bend or fit it—it's a whole lot stronger."

Such tricks of the trade came early to Henry, who apprenticed himself to wooden ships even though he grew up in the iron age. "Both my grandfathers was makin' ships, so I went in too. Did a lot of refittin' old yachts and such." Now a grandfather himself, Henry still relies on *his* grandfathers' handmade tools, many of which are wooden. "Made of wood, y'know, made to last. Use these tools every day—couldn't work without 'em."

Today, men like Henry are as rare as his heirloom tools. Few know the shipwright's ancient skills with the proper woods. No one makes wooden ships anymore. Even wooden boats are pretty much a thing of the past.

"It's all fiberglass and aluminum and that junk," grouses Henry. "But I guess you can't stop progress any more than you can stop the tides."

The same progress that stove in America's square-riggers doomed her maritime woodcarvings as well. Grand figureheads of mythological characters, talon-flexing eagles, and strong, flowing-robed maidens once endowed each vessel with an almost human individuality. But they disappeared with oaken ships, as did the fancily carved billetheads, sternboards, and shipboard expressions of man's lighter side, like scrimshaw. Woodcarvers found customers ashore, where their art provided everything from kitchen utensils to shop figures to those grand, overgrown toys we call carrousels.

The turn of the century capped the carrousel's golden age, when proud craftsmen patiently handcarved griffin chariots and jolly, lips-parted horses—each truly one of a kind. It was an age vitalized by highly skilled immigrants, men like Gustav Dentzel from the

More than any other natural resource, wood met the colonists' structural needs, from Jamestown's stockade to the stocks and pillory of Boston. The "goosewing" broadax below enabled settlers to shape rough-cut timbers rapidly and safely, its offset handle preventing the user from skinning or bruising his knuckles on his own work. Wood responded readily to this and other specialized hand tools of the day (opposite, from left): broadax, adz, auger, maul and chisel, handsaw, and plane. Artistic license crowds all six woodworkers elbow to elbow in this 19th-century engraving—itself a woodcut.

Rhineland and Salvatore Cernigliaro from Italy. Both were talented cabinetmakers drawn to the America of opportunity; both found carrousels more profitable than furniture.

Cernigliaro—better known as "Cherni"—worked in Dentzel's shop, winning praise for his intense, dynamic designs. Windswept manes and tight-muscled limbs make his horses far more bronco than saddle mare. Rampaging zebras paw the air; tigers snarl; deer brandish real antlers. Cherni's well-known White Rabbit doesn't crouch in trite bunny pose; it lopes with the grace of a gazelle. One ear thrusts up, the other flops down; a forepaw rises as if to wave hello. Carved tufts of "fur" blanket the body with detail. It is a Cherni masterpiece, wrought expertly from wood some 70 years ago.

Once whirling in a carrousel, the White Rabbit today stands stock-still on a pedestal at Heritage Plantation, a craft museum on Cape Cod. It and other survivors of now-defunct merry-go-rounds surround a restored carrousel built by Charles Looff. An immigrant cabinetmaker in the tradition of Cherni and Dentzel, Looff so loved carrousels that he carved a 54-horse extravaganza for his daughter's wedding gift.

I arrived at Heritage Plantation in autumn, when solitude had supplanted summer's joyful shrieks. The museum was all but deserted, its gaudy red-and-gold-trimmed carrousel closed for the season. But curator Bradley Smith delightedly put it in gear anyway and I, equally delighted, hopped on its whirling platform for a trip into the past.

It was a magical ride, this my first run on a carrousel since childhood. Perhaps it was the organ music's familiar ooom-pah-pah that first entranced me, or the hundreds of decorative mirrors that bounced the light around. Maybe it was the predictable, up-and-down race of my flaring-nostriled steed that summoned up visions from years gone by. Was it the thrill of straining for the brass ring? Slowly, I slipped into the warm cloak of nostalgia.

There's a time-machine effect to old carrousels, a bond to the past as warm as the feeling you get when you meet a long-lost friend. Carrousels breed nostalgia because they are reminders not only of a departed youth but also of an art form that died long ago.

As early as 1903, carving machines heralded the end of lavish handcrafted carrousels. Mass production swiftly led to the molded repetition of the Plastic Age. Carrousel horses

appeared in newer materials, as did ships, homes, furniture, and many other necessities.

Shop signs—a finely carved mortar and pestle for a druggist, a hanging wooden "ham" for a butcher—fell to the up-to-date appeal of printed signs and neon. Like the once-familiar cigar store Indian, woodcarving lapsed into the dusty attic of American crafts.

And yet in some things wood remains irreplaceable. No plastic can match its warmth, its grain, its feel, or its musical tone. Only wood can make a violin or piano.

Wood's unique property of tone will drive a fiddlemaker to pay a routine $100 for less than a pound of maple—enough to make only a single fiddleback. He pays because he believes a time-proved credo: You can't build a good violin from mediocre wood. The wood he seeks comes from special varieties of spruce and maple trees, harvested decades ago and slowly air-dried. Often the wood's age exceeds the violinmaker's!

But quality wood is only the beginning; a violinmaker must work his wood as skillfully as he picks it.

"Making musical instruments demands intuition as well as skill," says George D. Wilson, blond and lanky master instrument-maker at Colonial Williamsburg, Virginia. He speaks with more than twenty years' experience in the craft, at the age of 33. He makes harpsichords, lutes, guitars, and viola da gambas as well as violins.

"You can take a piece of furniture apart, see how it was made, and copy it easily—that takes technological skill. But with instruments, you need something more. You need to build in fine tone."

That 'tone' can be elusive. Generations of violinmakers have failed to equal the best Stradivarius and Amati violins, built in the 17th and 18th centuries and still coveted as the world's finest. Wood responds to the vibrations of music with a growing mellowness of tone; but no formula explains what makes these violins so good.

"There are a lot of fallacies," Wilson cautions. "Some say the old masters had unique varnishes or special glues or something. Well, I'm sure they didn't. Everyone chose from the same materials; some just picked theirs better." Stradivarius had "a phenomenal gift" for selecting woods, Wilson believes, in the same way that great chefs consistently concoct masterpieces from the meats and vegetables available to others.

Wilson's own recipe for selecting wood smacks of wizardry. How does he know which boards will make an exceptional violin?

"It's a *feeling* I get. I look for a certain texture, a hardness, a *complexion* to the wood. I'll tap it and listen for a clear ring. It's really a combination of all the aspects, something you know only from experience."

Experience—as musician and woodworker—also tells Wilson to work these boards gently. "You've got to take off wood very slowly, maybe 1/32 of an inch at a time, and let the wood 'rest' between takes. That way, the shock to the wood isn't so great; it helps prevent warping. That's one reason why hand tools are better than machines—they're slower."

As Wilson's wood slowly metamorphoses into musical instrument, he taps it again and again, letting its tone guide his next move. "Feel" and experience tell him where to trim, when to stop.

Sometimes, lavish decoration crowns the work. Intricate carvings and pierced work, rich inlays of holly, ebony, and other woods dance across lute, guitar, and harpsichord. Sometimes a dozen different woods color a single instrument.

"Everything I make is one of a kind. The combination of woods, the inlay work and other decorations all vary from piece to piece, because I don't like to do the same thing time after time."

Each creation gives Wilson a tremendous satisfaction. A violin or viola da gamba made to his exacting standards is more than an assemblage of expertly carved and fitted parts that will outlive its maker. It is more than warm, elegantly grained wood laced with hairline inlays, more than a wellspring of rich melodies. It is a functional work of art.

Not only beautiful but playable, such a violin embodies the ultimate union of man's skill and wood's unique personality. It is everything that wood can be.

And yet, the violinmaker shares the skills basic to all quality craftsmen of wood. Like Nakashima and Cherni, like the famed cabinetmakers and the nameless coopers, wheelwrights, joiners and other craftsmen of necessity in America's past, George Wilson merges with wood in a common effort to achieve the uncommon. His basic fiber, like theirs, drives him ever to bring his best talents to wood, to respect wood's spirit and mold it with the excellence traditional to craftsmen bred in the American grain.

Wood's manifold uses made it a household necessity even in mansions built of brick. No wealthy family of the 18th century lacked for wooden wig stands (above). Some also used carved molds to decorate marzipan cakes. Below, eagles and stars flank an equestrian George Washington, testimony to the outbursts of patriotism that swept post-Revolutionary crafts.

Colonists called it "treen"—meaning "of the tree"
—but Indians created America's first woodenware,
such as a mortar and pestle probably used to grind
corn. Surviving treenware made by the settlers includes a watertight bowl of burl maple, dated
1791, and a Pilgrim grain measure, a round
board nailed to a hollowed-out section of tree trunk.

ACTUAL SIZE: C. 17 INCHES HIGH

NATIONAL GEOGRAPHIC PHOTOGRAPHER BATES LITTLEHALES

11 INCHES LONG

13½ INCHES IN DIAMETER

High-speed lathes and silky lacquers help bowlmaker Bob Stocksdale of California achieve a grace in wood impossible for earlier craftsmen. Shielded by a plastic faceplate, guided only by eye and experience, this power-tool sculptor designs each bowl or tray right on the lathe, "reading" the grain as he goes. A distinctive grain rules not only the shape of the piece but also the contours of its lip (above). This bowl of blackwood acacia—one of the maker's favorites—highlights a touring show of Stocksdale creations: 77 one-of-a-kind bowls and trays, made from 44 kinds of wood, native and exotic.

America's chairs, like her settlers, developed from European origins. Duncan Phyfe's mahogany sidechair with reeded legs (far left), made in 1807, adapts designs current in London. The mahogany chair beside it interprets 1850's fashion for a plantation parlor—the work of North Carolina's Tom Day, who sold such chairs at $45 a dozen!

New England's first furniture imitated the mother country's; and many craftsmen copied the robust armchair (above) made for Elder William Brewster of Plymouth. English sturdiness also marks the country highchair designed to hold a wriggling child without tipping.

But American chairmakers gave a new lightness to their ladderback, Windsor, and Shaker styles (opposite, left to right). This big ladderback shows the trend beginning; its owner Jonathan Copp called it "my great chair" in a will dated 1746, and the original top slat has lost its curved crest. Windsors consistently reflect even more airiness, as do the simple Shaker chairs—purely American.

Heir to styles so varied, self-taught woodworker Sam Maloof of California creates his own designs, such as the spindle-back rocker (far right). Of all cabinetry, Sam finds chairmaking "the most time-consuming—there are so many joints it's like working a jigsaw puzzle."

Showcase for 20th-century modern, Sam Maloof's dining room merges redwood paneling and walnut furniture, all the work of the owner. The bowls came from friend and fellow craftsman Bob Stocksdale, in exchange for a Maloof chair.

LOWELL GEORGIA

Styles for 19th-century living range from Shaker (above) to opulent Victorian (right). Abhorring useless decoration as idle clutter, Shakers evolved strictly functional designs, usually in maple, pine, or cherry. But Victorians preferred darker wood, rich decor. German-born William Bartels, an Illinois farmer who began woodworking while recovering from typhoid, labored years on a 22-item suite that includes this dolphin-legged oak table. He never sold any of these pieces; legend says he rejected a million-dollar offer from Queen Victoria herself.

At Old Sturbridge Village, cabinetmaker R. E. Bushnell reproduces a Queen Anne highboy.

Furniture of early America evolved within regional boundaries. An oak-and-pine chest (far left) attributed to 17th-century joiner Thomas Dennis bears painted floral carvings common in New England. Wax-and-lead inlay decorates a Pennsylvania Dutch "shrank" or wardrobe of walnut. A mahogany high chest with flame finials represents 18th-century "Philadelphia Chippendale" from a center of wealth and fashion. The city's craftsmen gained lasting fame for carved details like the mahogany bas-relief above, from an 1827 secretary in the Empire style.

By subtle modeling or expressive emphasis, Indian carvers characterized their ceremonial masks. On a cedar mask collected about 1840, a labret, or pierced-lip ornament, proclaims high status for a Tlingit woman of the Pacific Northwest. Tribes of this region brought masterly skill to objects as varied as small charms or totem poles. For healing rituals, the Iroquois still cut from living basswood their horsehair-topped masks like that at right; it represents a supernatural being with power to cause and cure so-called "false face sicknesses."

In the Great Southwest, wood has served religious purposes for both Hopi Indian and Christian settler. Yearly, in Hopi rites, masked dancers impersonate kachinas—mountain-dwelling spirits who take prayers to the gods. Heirs to ritual craftwork centuries old, fathers and uncles carve kachina dolls in tight-grained cottonwood root; dancers present them to daughters and nieces. This doll symbolizes Ma-alo, a bringer of rain

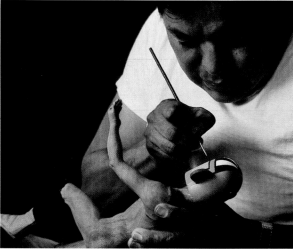

TERRY EILER

and bountiful corn tasseling. Carvers like Alvin James Makya (above, painting the facial markings of a "social dancer") make kachina dolls in the traditional style for ceremonies and more detailed, realistic ones for sale to collectors.

ACTUAL HEIGHT, 8 INCHES

Such carvers as José Mondragón (below) continue the Spanish folk practice of making bultos—religious figures in the round. Mondragón's aspen-wood rendering of St. Peter with the keys of heaven contrasts with the baroque St. Michael (right), the work of soldier-sculptor Bernardo Miera y Pacheco in 1776. The shield gives in Latin the meaning of the archangel's name: "Who is like God?" Brightly painted and

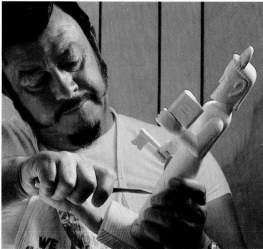

NATIONAL GEOGRAPHIC PHOTOGRAPHER OTIS IMBODEN

gilded, such statues inspired unschooled colonists to make simplified figures for home shrines. After 1850, Roman Catholic reformers frowned on the bultos as crude and unsuitable, and urged the faithful to discard them.

ACTUAL HEIGHT, 38 INCHES

Tobacconist's trademark, the cigar-store Indian carried a message the illiterate could understand: smoke shop here. Styles varied widely, from the stern Indian woman at upper right, believed the work of a slave, to a mirthful Punch. A handful of cigars ensured the right interpretation. Black-face entertainer Thomas D. Rice, famed as "Jim Crow," generated a 19th-century fad of songs, hats, and carvings—including the figure opposite.

Famed or obscure or anonymous, figure carvers have enriched many American buildings. For more than a century, Father Time has counted the Maiden's ringlets atop the Masonic Temple in Mendocino, California; the broken pillar represents work halted by death. Builder Eric Albertson shaped these in local redwood. Carved about 1828 for Philadelphia's new waterworks, a Grecian head proves the exceptional skill of William Rush. Silversmith and cabinetmaker of Revolutionary times, John Fisher produced a blindfolded Justice for a Pennsylvania courtroom. A folk-art study in character, the woman riding sidesaddle advertised a ladies' bootery in the early 1860's.

DETAIL

Still spirited after decades of disuse, a galloping carrousel horse and a snarling pride of lions on the side of an old-time circus wagon recall a golden age of America's amusement industry. Economic depression in 19th-century Europe prompted many woodcarvers to bring their skills to the United States. From the 1880's through the early 1900's, rival American companies — many led by master carvers — produced ever-grander, flashier carrousels and circuses. But just as the shop figure vanished when fashion changed, so the carrousel succumbed to mass production. After 1903, carving machines began to supplant maul-and-chisel sculptors; soon, plastics replaced wood itself. Thousands of one-of-a-kind woodcarvings wasted into decay. Some — like the circus wagon below — survive through the work of restorers at Circus World Museum in Baraboo, Wisconsin. Others find sanctuary in private collections. Cabinetmaker Sam Maloof owns — and his grandchildren ride — this horse, now stripped of old paint to show off its joinery and weathered grain of poplar.

WINGSPREAD 11⅛ INCHES

WINGSPREAD 6⅜ INCHES

WINGSPREAD 36½ INCHES

WINGSPREAD 4 FEET 7¼ INCHES

Motif of patriot craftsmen, the eagle spreads its wings in wood. Eagles in inlay grace the back of a newly remodeled banjo and the oval seal made about 1797 for the Speaker's Desk in Maryland's state capitol. Two eagles in relief, one shown above, have ridden a circus bandwagon since 1905. At least one clockmaker chose an eagle for his shop sign. The national bird often appeared on merchant ships. A steamboat's eagle (below) floated ashore after an 1865 shipwreck ripped it from the paddlewheel box. Wilhelm Schimmel of Pennsylvania, a vagabond whittler well-known to jails and almshouses, carved the statue at left—one of many he bartered for food, shelter, and the whisky that contributed to what a local newspaper termed his "very surly disposition."

WINGSPREAD 40 INCHES

WINGSPREAD 6 FEET

55

Birds of the hand: America's indigenous art of decoy-making began at least 1,000 years ago with Indian lures of woven reeds and stuffed bird skins. Colonists whittled their own counterfeits from wood. Stylized in form and color, decoys imitated almost any gregarious bird valued as food: the now-extinct passenger pigeon (right) or the mallard (center) and curlew (far right), both now protected by law. Today, mass-produced Styrofoam decoys cost about $20 per dozen, yet many hunters choose to pay $15 for a single factory-made wooden bird. They prefer the way wood rides in the water. Handmade ornamental models appeal to collectors. Many especially prize decoys by Lem Ward (below) or his brother Steve of Crisfield, Maryland, two notable craftsmen now virtually retired. Famed for

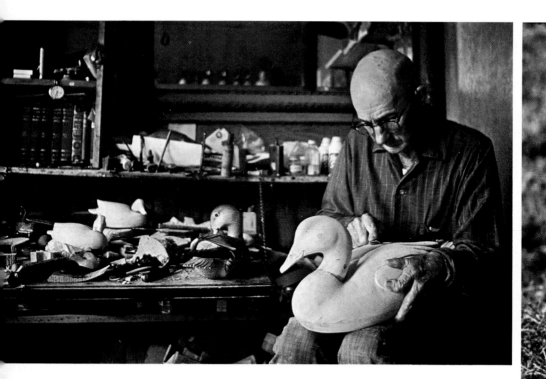

feather-by-feather realism, Lem Ward birds like these Canada geese might fetch thousands of dollars apiece—quite a jump from the $18 a dozen the Wards charged for "working" decoys soon after they started to carve in 1918.

Williamsburg's George D. Wilson completes a new violin, and Clarence Berger of Washington, D. C., finishes the scrollwork, a job he finds "one of the hardest parts—and it's just decoration." First of all, he says, "you must have the right, the best, wood, or you're wasting your time." "Made as a violin and played as a fiddle—for hoedowns," says Ozarks carver J. R. McNeill of the gleaming instrument above. The first he has made, it "took a year's spare time." Short of cash and craftsmanship but eager for music and fun, some mountain musicians in the past would fiddle on dried gourds like the one below.

Handcrafted scale replicas of whaler Kate Cory *(below) and the Pilgrims'*
Mayflower *(lower right) permit an accuracy impossible in mass production.
"They're as much scholarly pursuit as craft," says mini-shipwright Erik Ronnberg,
Jr., of Rockport, Massachusetts. He devoted some 2,000 hours to researching* Kate
Cory's *little-known past and drawing up plans, another 600 to carving, fitting,
and rigging this model. His devotion to detail requires woods that resemble scaled-
down versions of the originals, even in grain. Thus tight-grained holly provides
"oak" planking. Such painstaking methods stem from a model-building father,
who inspired the younger Ronnberg to complete his first effort (right) at age six.*

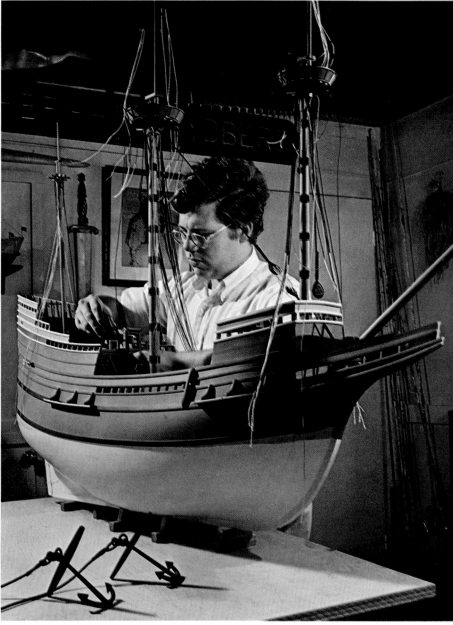

Keeping up with the Casey Joneses: Adult rail buffs throughout the country devote themselves to toy trains. But few can boast anything like this precisely-to-scale model locomotive and tender of the New York, New Haven & Hartford line. James C. Norton, with a talent for woodcarving and a lot of time, built this marvel in 1908, using wood even for the rivetheads, side rods, and bell and clapper. Its size— actual length, 28 inches— allowed accuracy in wooden wheels and other mechanical parts that move like their counterparts in metal. A railroad man himself, curator of the Edaville Railroad Museum in South Carver, Massachusetts, Ralph E. Fisher calls this "a whittler's masterpiece—the best I ever saw made of wood."

"I've tried all kinds of wood," says sculptor David Hostetler of Ohio; "elm, box elder, and walnut now top my list." At right, he completes "Nella," a "symbolic portrait" of a client's wife in rare chestnut. He chose willow for "Flare Skirt" (left) and walnut for "Maid of Nantucket," named for his summer haunt. He describes the Maid as "a blend of an East Coast ship's figure and folk carvings of the Midwest."

NATIONAL GEOGRAPHIC PHOTOGRAPHER BATES LITTLEHALES

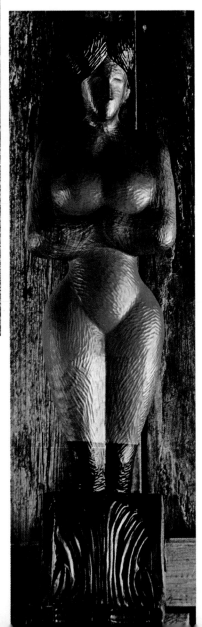

A Nautical

OF ALL WOODCRAFT, shipbuilding ranks as one of the oldest arts—and certainly one vital to progress in the New World from colonial days onward. Shipwrights learned their indispensable trade by apprenticeship, as did other marine craftsmen: riggers and sailmakers, ship's carpenters, who kept vessels in good repair, and ship carvers.

From the British "lyon" of the 17th century to the emblems and heroes of the independent United States, carvings recorded and symbolized changes in American life.

Apart from such skilled professionals as the ship carver, seamen indulged in handicrafts as maritime hobbies. Tedium plagued most voyages, and few sailors had books on board; crafts busied their minds and hands off watch —or even on watch in fair weather.

Whittling was popular, for every sailor carried a jackknife. The world's ports offered him mahogany, teak, and other exotic woods. From wood he might progress to whale teeth

Portfolio

BY TOM MELHAM

or bone, the prized materials for scrimshaw.

Knowing the ropes in the literal sense, for knotting and splicing, led naturally to decorative ropework as a pastime. Mats and netting, handles for sea chests, curtains and dust ruffles for gifts—all grew out of the sailor's skill with knots.

Just as each able-bodied seaman could splice a halyard, he could mend sails or his own clothes. His callused hands, expert at basic sewing, mastered projects as varied as delicate embroidery for loved ones or tobacco pouches sewn from the leathery webbing of seabirds' feet.

Always, handicaps beset the seaborne folk artist. Usually he worked as an amateur, devising tools as needed. His studio was an open deck or a cramped fo'c'sle; one jostling shipmate, one roll of the ship, might spoil his labor of months. And yet he persevered, patiently working his assorted materials into jewels of the storied Age of Sail.

Figureheads of Pacific waters still serve a port of call—as displays at the San Francisco Maritime Museum. Used in the California trade, clipper David Crockett *carried a namesake carving on board, but not at the bow. Considered one of the rare figureheads carved on the West Coast, the eagle above clung 44 years to the prow of the barkentine* Charles F. Crocker, *named for the magnate who helped complete America's first transcontinental railroad. Demand for ship's carvings ran high; the trade card below promised "Models of any kind executed at shortest notice."*

"Sailor's valentine" sets dainty shells in a mock-floral arrangement—a symbol of love that Nantucket whaling captain Jared Tracy brought home to his wife, Mary, about 1840. He had survived a shipwreck in the Indian Ocean; family tradition holds that the anchor implied he would "anchor at her side" for good. The delicate workmanship may seem out of character for a whaling skipper, but sailors admired anything so skillfully done. Even embroidery, as in the crewel seascape below, won their acclaim. Working knots like the "manrope" knot (opposite, top) might appear on a sea-chest handle. Such knots, tinkered with in off-hours, blossomed into inventions used today by macramé artists and rope sculptors. Seamen linked their knots into lavish fancywork that might decorate a seabag, a chest, or a berth.

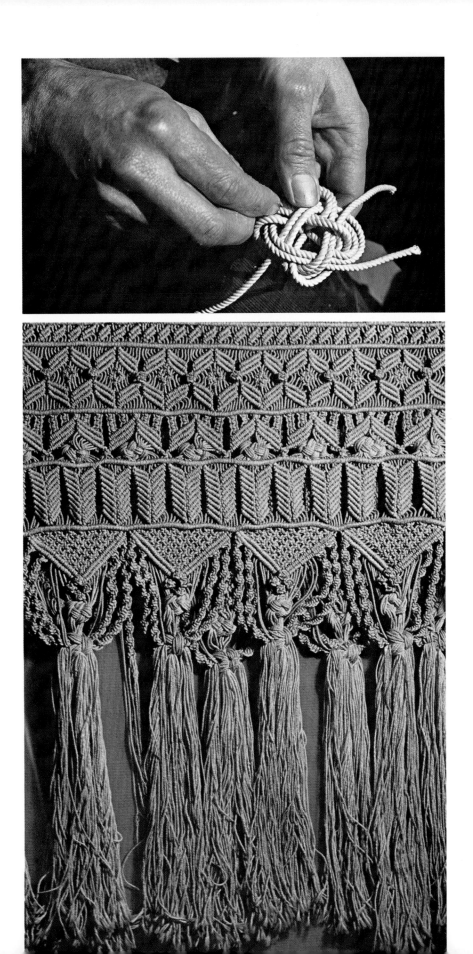

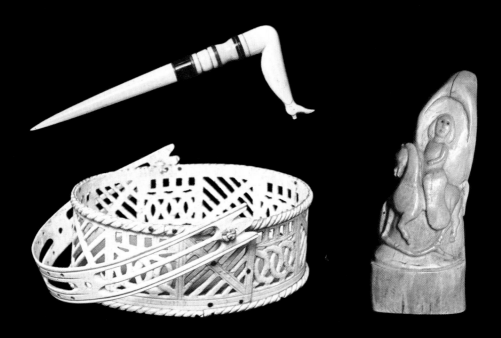

Scrimshaw — the working of whale teeth and bone — began as the sailor's answer to idle hours at sea. With jackknife, sail needle, and imagination, he fashioned marvels in ivory: a seamstress's bodkin above a basket of bone, a bas-relief, a portrait, a sinuous pastry crimper. Scrimshaw's diversity demanded the skills of a good carver, joiner, turner, engraver, and inlayer. It also demanded unlimited time — time to scrape the tooth clean, time to polish it with sharkskin or ashes, time to incise a design and bring it out with India ink or soot or dye. Women and whaling themes predominate (below). These pieces range from an 1829 antique

(far left) to contemporary scrim-shander William Gilkerson's study of the whaler Gay Head *(below and right). Despite such current accomplishments in scrimshaw, the art may die out: The government now bans whale products from import, because the great whales face extinction.*

3

From the American Earth

LIVING FOR MORE THAN TWO YEARS in an Indian village northeast of Bombay, I learned to appreciate the work of local craftsmen in the most direct of ways—by using its products, as other villagers had done for centuries. I carried water from the village well in a brass *lota*, and savored the coolness water acquires by standing in an unglazed earthenware jar.

I have struggled to gain some skill of my own at a potter's wheel; and have visited factories where machinery supplements handwork, such as the Iron Mountain Stoneware plant at Laurel Bloomery, Tennessee.

All these experiences come back to me when I look at examples of the native ceramics of America. And I am amazed at the symmetry and delicacy of these objects, formed with the craftsman's most ancient tools, his hands and his eyes.

The earth itself supplies the most basic material, a suitable clay. Probably every potter worth the name develops a feeling for its properties. Tony Da, a successful young potter of San Ildefonso Pueblo, New Mexico, conveys it vividly in speaking of his grandmother and teacher, the famed Maria Martinez: "When we would go to the pits to dig clay, she would pull out a little pouch of cornmeal and sprinkle it over the earth, silently praying and blessing the earth before she took from it."

In times beyond memory, throughout the continent, Indian potters coiled snakelike lengths of clay into basic shapes. They blended these into smooth, thin-walled vessels with their fingers or with smooth stones ("anvils") and wooden paddles.

They left many pieces plain, but they achieved decoration by varied methods: incising lines with a sharp stick, pressing the crinkled edge of a shell along a rim, stamping designs into the moist clay with carved or cloth-wrapped paddles. Such devices added texture. Color came from pigments like red ocher or soot or creamy-white clay.

Firing gives clay the hardness that makes it useful. It also gives the potter a relentless test of skill—and luck. Even with the use of a brick-lined kiln, it creates a tension that the noted potter Charles Counts of Rising Fawn, Georgia, calls an "ecstasy of hope and fear."

Indian potters relied on a bed of hot coals in the open, a tricky procedure. They placed their wares on supports like stones or potsherds, shielded them with more sherds, and covered them with bark or wood or dried animal dung to secure a hotter, more even burn. Wind-blown flame may scorch a pot; too little heat may warp it; too much heat may break it.

"If I fail it hurts," says Juanita C. Arquero, of Cochiti Pueblo; for a good firing, "I'm thankful to God for my skill."

The plainest earthenware pot is a technical victory; the best Indian decoration is an artistic triumph of sophistication.

Early European explorers and settlers had contact with pottery-making tribes, and commented with some interest on the curious shapes of their cooking vessels. But though colonists were willing to learn about planting corn, they made no attempt to borrow Indian ceramic forms or motifs. Potters from Europe kept to their own tradition and their own basic devices: wheel and kiln.

As early as 1635, the first English potters arrived in Massachusetts. Settlers at Jamestown, Virginia, were probably producing pottery already. By 1800, there were more than 250 potters in New England alone, usually running a small family enterprise.

Like many of his fellow artisans, the colonial potter had to do or direct all the work for a single piece—a time-consuming process. And

Seeking "a synthesis of clay and form and fire and spirit," Georgian Charles Counts coaxes from his clay the graceful lines of a pitcher.

By Andy Leon Harney

LOWELL GEORGIA

often he was a farmer or fisherman as well.

The potter could dig for clay in the fall, searching it out by lakes or streams. Its quality conditioned what he could make. Redware predominated in colonial New England, because local clays would yield little else.

He would haul his clay home—"a great quantity of the stuff is needed," says Counts dryly—and pick out all the gravel and twigs. He would break it up, wash it, perhaps several times, make it into large balls for storage and seasoning. Sooner or later he would divide it into smaller units and knead it thoroughly to prepare it for throwing.

"Throwing a pot" sounded odd to me until I tried it. You must slam the clay onto the wheel head to make it stick. Otherwise you watch it sail right out of your hands after the first few turns of the wheel! And you must "center" the clay—place its center directly over that of the wheel head—or find yourself facing an elliptical bowl, a wobbly plate.

Colonial potters used a kick-wheel or a treadle to propel the wheel head; many potters today use the same basic device because they enjoy the direct control it gives. Whatever the source of power, achieving a correct rhythm in the wheel is crucial.

I remember trying involuntarily to follow the wheel around with my hands, instead of keeping them still while the wheel turned beneath my fingers. I felt like a novice driver in a car going too fast downhill as the wheel picked up speed and I lost control. I put my foot down hard to stop the whirligig in front of me—only to force my centered cylinder into a distorted ellipse.

I sympathize with any colonial apprentice who made the same mistake and created a shape with no market value. And I can see why the apprentice would get the simpler task of pulling handles for cups or jugs or chamberpots—you pull the clay with much the same motion you use to milk a cow.

To make a profit with relatively cheap ware, a potter had to produce as much as possible; and he could easily lose all the work invested in it if something went wrong in the firing.

He would need wagonloads of wood, properly aged and dry. He would arrange his wares in the kiln, handling the brittle stuff gently, packing it as close as safety permitted. (A piece fired too damp can explode when heated and send its flying fragments into the wares arranged around it.) He would tend his fire as long as 36 hours to raise the heat—

to about 1,800° F. for earthenware—and control his impatience for another 36 hours or more while the kiln cooled. If he opened it too soon, the abrupt change of temperature would crack or shatter the contents.

Only when a purchaser has bought a vessel can the maker enjoy the sentiment that a Pennsylvania German inscribed on a plate: "The dish is made of earth;/When it breaks the potter laughs."

Beyond the natural uncertainties of clay and fire, the colonial potter—like other craftsmen of his time—worked under adversities of political origin. By policy and statute, Great Britain discouraged any development of industry in her colonies; she wanted to sell them goods made in the home islands. This may have confused the historical record more than it deterred the craftsmen in America.

Repeatedly, in the 1730's, Governor William Gooch of Virginia assured the Board of Trade in London that the one "poor Potter" in Yorktown was "unworthy of your Lordships notice"—making nothing but cheap items for "the poorest Familys."

But archeologists Ivor Noël Hume and Norman Barka have proved that the Yorktown pottery was a sizable factory; and Noël Hume calls some of its ware "very accomplished—equal in quality to the English." Moreover, historian Malcolm Watkins has identified the "poor Potter" as one William Rogers, first described as "brewer" in local records but later as "merchant" or "gent." Rogers died well-to-do; his estate, valued at £1,224, included 31 slaves; and Watkins labels him "Mr. Upward Mobility himself."

Governor Gooch, adds Watkins, "knew the art of the cover-up!" Gooch was very popular in Virginia; obviously he saw that the realities of colonial life demanded such expansion in local craft and trade.

In the 1750's colonial pottery was coming into its own, emphasizing regional character and selling in quantity. The Pennsylvania Germans were producing more and more of their bright earthenware. They colored it with slip, a thin wash of clay; scratched designs into the surface, a technique called sgrafitto; and often added homilies or proverbs in German.

Probably a bachelor inscribed the dish that says: "Rather would I single live / Than the wife the breeches give." A woman signed her work gravely: "Catherine Raeder, her dish, / Out of the earth with understanding / The potter makes everything."

By 1785 people were beginning to understand the hazards of lead glazes that brought out the gay reds and yellows of slip decoration and made dishwashing easier. Acid foods—sauerkraut, pickles, cider—would leach out the lead. A notice in the *Pennsylvania Mercury* warned that this lead acted as "a slow but sure poison" to the nervous system, causing "paleness, tremors, gripes, palsies &c." The writer urged American legislatures to encourage the production of "Stone-ware" with its "perfect and wholesome glazing, produced only from SAND and SALTS."

Common salt will indeed form a perfect glaze, given suitable clays containing silica and techniques of firing them at temperatures as high as 2,300°. At such heat, the clay itself acquires a glassy quality with or without salt. But I learned when I visited the Iron Mountain plant, which produces unglazed stoneware, that even today skilled workers can lose as much as 25 percent of their ware in the complex process.

Yet a few colonial potters—including William Rogers of Yorktown!—found appropriate clays and mastered ways of high-firing; stoneware became increasingly popular in the United States, especially for storing food.

Even in the 19th century, however, American potters felt the competition of European china; and in a pinch, people who could not afford any pottery could always use woodenware as the earliest settlers had often done.

Although pioneers could make do without a local potter, the blacksmith's craft was essential to every settlement. Without the tools made and kept in repair by the blacksmith, a man could not bring crops from the earth. The housewife's hearth needed a pot and kettle and spit. Ax blades for cutting wood, chains for hauling it, nails for securing it—the smith and his forge were indispensable.

"He was working in wrought iron," explains contemporary metalsmith Michael Jerry, "and he could forge and weld it easily. What's more difficult is bending it without breaking it; it has a fibrous structure—like wood."

In the South, many blacksmiths were indentured servants or slaves, especially in plantation country. There—and in other rural regions—the smith might do farrier's work: making shoes for horses and fitting them on.

That blurs the lines of a craft distinction, as veteran blacksmith Stewart Fahnstrom makes plain. Today he does custom work for the restored Swedish pioneer settlement at Bishop

Foot treadle turns a potter's wheel in a 19th-century woodcut. American pottery in the 1800's took diverse forms. Bulbous eyes peer from an effigy jug, probably by a black potter in South Carolina. A bearded face decorates a stoneware jug from New York. Lead glazes for earthenware appear on a green jug and a red jar with an unusual pinched middle—both from New England.

Banner of painted silk waved above the patriotic pewterers of New York City as they marched in the Federal Procession of July 23, 1788, celebrating the ratification of the Constitution.

Hill, Illinois; in World War I he served with the American Expeditionary Force in France.

"I was in the Argonne drive, and the captain said to me, 'You shoe horses?' 'Captain, I don't know a thing about shoeing horses— there's a big difference between a blacksmith and a horse shoer.' He said I ought to be able to weld toe caulks and turn heel caulks and fit the shoes. I said, 'You bet I can!' 'Then do it.'—So I did it."

The blacksmith was always a man of versatility. In a capital like Williamsburg, blacksmiths might repair surgical instruments and carriages. They doubled as gunsmiths and armorers, making ramrods for muskets.

In Michael Jerry's opinion, metalcraft distinctions of colonial days owe more to Old World habit than to the nature of the metals themselves; and he works with a full range of them at his studio in Syracuse, New York. Trained as a silversmith, he has turned to iron with enthusiasm. "The techniques for metals are closely related," he says, "and they all differ from the potter's.

"Generally, you can predict what metals will do—the potter's always praying over the kiln. But you can be more spontaneous shaping clay. The metalworker has to think it through before he starts."

Obtaining the raw materials gave some colonial metalworkers a good deal to think about and grumble at. The tinsmith had to buy sheet metal from England. The colonists discovered iron ore as early as 1607 and worked it—regulations after 1683 to the contrary—until the Revolution, but the country has never yielded adequate deposits of tin.

Tinsmiths were few in the early 18th century, when Shem Drowne made weather vanes in Boston; by the early 19th, one smith noted, Yankee tin peddlers were "thick as toads after a rain." Their ware had real advantages—tin utensils weigh less than iron, and a shiny surface lets unpainted tin share with pewter the tag of "poor man's silver."

Legend notwithstanding, silver has no place in pewter alloys. Tin is the essential element, and the best pewter is more than 90 percent tin. Copper or bismuth or antimony adds strength to the metal. Lead makes it easier to work; much pewter contained at least 5 percent lead, the cheapest grades as much as 40.

Even so, a colonial craftsman could buy a pewter tankard or dish with a day's earnings when its silver counterpart would easily cost him a full month's; pewter was "finery," a token of gentility.

To protect the pewterers of England, the Board of Trade prohibited the export of pure tin and taxed the unworked alloy but not the finished vessels.

But pewter, though easily dented or damaged by direct heat, lends itself to recycling, routine for all metals in the past. The American pewterer had a lively trade in melting down old ware and making new items—"nice and new and shiny," as Michael Jerry says.

Essential steps of his craft appear in the only known American picture of an 18th-century pewter shop, a painting on the silk banner carried by the New York Society of Pewterers in a grand procession that celebrated the adoption of the Constitution. At the left, a workman is apparently casting molten metal. One man turns a wheel lathe for a colleague "skimming" or scraping smooth a plate. In the foreground a man hardens a dish with a planishing hammer—a standard tool for silversmiths but used only for the finest grades of pewter.

Completed items on the banner include the familiar teapot and tankards, but the shield gives pride of place to the neat coils of a distiller's worm for making whiskey!

Such complicated gear would require a skilled craftsman, but tinkers and householders could—and did—mold pewter spoons or buttons. The professional pewterer often bought old metal; and the silversmith had an even more important role in this respect.

In a country without banks, and with a perennial shortage of currency, silver offered a man of means a safe and stable investment. It confirmed his social standing even as it gave splendor to his table.

Of course in some respects the investment depended on the integrity of the smith. Pure silver melts readily, at 1,761° F. An unscrupulous smith could make a stolen porringer or caudle cup as unrecognizable as stolen coin. In the Old World, guilds governed and policed the craftsmen of precious metals. But, says historian of silver Kathryn C. Buhler, "we may proudly note that our goldsmiths were under no supervision and rarely needed any."

Styling themselves "goldsmiths," although they usually worked in the less valuable metal, seems the worst charge that can be brought

DETAIL

Portrayed in his Boston workshop in the late 1760's, silversmith Paul Revere contemplates a teapot before engraving it. Artist John Singleton Copley, in a notable departure from the convention of his time, showed him at work in his shirtsleeves. An activist for American rights, Revere honored patriot legislators with this silver punch-bowl, commissioned in 1768 by local Sons of Liberty. Routine creations included jewelry like the gold-and-enamel mourning ring set with an amethyst, and a silver-on-copper shoe buckle that recalls his pioneering role in the copper industry of the United States.

against these colonial masters. From the 17th century on, men like Jeremiah Dummer and John Coney in New England, or Jacob Boelen and Cornelis vander Burch in New York, set high standards for their apprentices.

Probably some did less than ideal work. "Don't think all those colonial silversmiths were perfect craftsmen, not by a long shot," says a Williamsburg smith of today, James Curtis, who uses the techniques and tools of his 18th-century predecessors. "For one thing, sometimes they made blobby solder joints."

More than probably, some less skilled work vanished with some of the best, melted down as fashions changed. Old silver was often the material of "new," along with that standard ingredient, foreign coins: pieces of eight, pistareens, "dog dollars" from the Netherlands.

When General George Washington ordered a set of 12 "camp cups" from Edmond Milne of Philadelphia, he sent the metal: "16 silv^r Doll^s"—perhaps Spanish milled dollars minted in Mexico. Milne kept the 1¾ ounces left over, carefully credited against his fee.

Undoubtedly America's most famous silversmith is Paul Revere of Boston. If Henry Wadsworth Longfellow made him a figure of myth, the patriot rider of midnight, Revere's own activities secure his place in craft history.

A man of enormous energy, he had a wide array of skills by age 35. Aside from his regular gold and silverwork, which included "taking out bruises" in dented pieces, he could "rivit" broken china or fix false teeth that were "not only an Ornament, but of real use in Speaking and Eating." A master of engraving on silver, he had less skill at his self-taught trade of engraving on copper plate; but he could serve the patriot cause with both.

After completing his famous "Sons of Liberty" punchbowl in 1768, to acclaim 92 patriot legislators, he attacked 17 others whose vote had pleased the King. He made an engraving that shows them entering, to use the title he chose, "A Warm Place—Hell."

In the Revolutionary War his state gave him the all-important task of learning how gunpowder should be made. After the war, he learned how to roll sheet copper and make spikes and other copper fastenings for ships— a "technological breakthrough" for the navy. He became a cannon founder, too. He learned to cast church bells "complimented . . . for their good and pleasing sound," as he proudly noted—as exacting a task as any in metallurgy.

In those bustling postwar years, the silversmith's craft began to change, with the use of rolled sheet silver of uniform thickness. This offered the option of shaping vessels by bending and seaming the metal, not by hammerwork alone. Hammering, the fundamental process of colonial silvercraft, is much slower and more complex—a master might own as many as 116 hammers.

Though his techniques changed, Revere's best designs remained superb. The "Revere pitcher," still popular in reproductions, modifies an English earthenware pitcher into a classic of silverwork. He rendered Chinese porcelain bowls in silver with equal success. And he kept a classical restraint in tea or coffee services after the prevailing fashion.

In this he maintained an American tradition. Colonial silver—and pewter—had habitually followed London styles, with some time lag. But often the American smiths used less ornament and produced simpler items, graceful of form and serviceable. On silver as on other metals and on pottery, life in the New World set its own stamp.

Between novel conditions and established styles and the timeless properties of his material, the craftsman learned by his mistakes and achieved his successes.

Copley's portrait of Revere combines the important elements of the process. A new informality of pose. Details of a craft: the small sand-filled bag that steadies the piece and protects the polished metal from scratches; the teapot's wooden handle that protects the hand from the heat of boiling water; the engraver's burin. Attributes of a craftsman: the alert eyes, the strong wrists, the broken fingernails of working hands.

How a shape fits the hand; how a metal transfers heat; how a vessel looks in sunlight —the contemporary American designer Charles Eames has discussed just such questions in analyzing the ancient, everyday lota of the villages in India. Eames considered the same factors that concerned the colonial housewife and the metalsmith—how heavy is a vessel, how strong are the hands that use it? And factors that concerned the potter, Indian or white—what this vessel will hold and how easily it can be cleaned; how it would be to own this piece, or to give it away.

Craft returns us to fundamentals. And its products, from silver pitcher to horseshoe to earthenware pot, reflect this. Charles Counts has given currency to an old phrase for it: "the majesty of the essential."

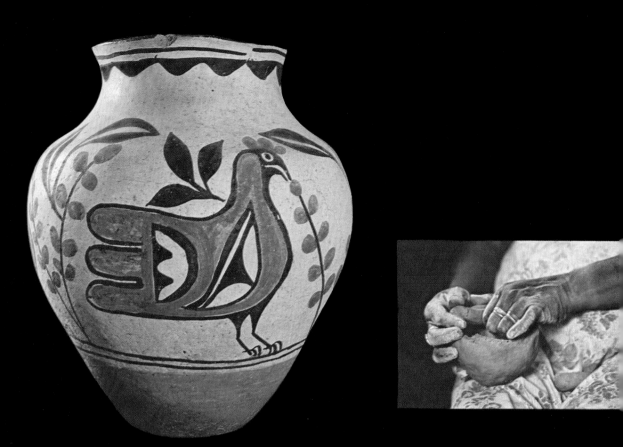

Layering inch-thick coils of clay, a Hopi Indian in Arizona fashions a pot by the technique used in the jar from Santo Domingo Pueblo, New Mexico. Pennsylvania Germans produced earthenware such as David Spinner's plate; at Old Salem, North Carolina, Rufus Matthews demonstrates their basic tool, the potter's wheel.

NATIONAL GEOGRAPHIC PHOTOGRAPHER OTIS IMBODEN (BELOW AND OPPOSITE)

TERRY EILER (ABOVE)

Heat gives strength and durability to clay during the firing process. Wearing a red bandanna, Juanita Arquero of Cochiti Pueblo in New Mexico examines some of the boldly patterned pots she has just fired on a stone hearth at temperatures that reach 1,400° F. At sunrise on a windless day, Hopi potter Rachael Nampeyo of Arizona builds a fire of sheep dung; she will bury her preheated pots in the coals for four or five hours. In her studio at Garrison, Maryland, Mary Nyburg checks a stoneware pot before firing it in a brick-walled kiln. Overleaf: Mary closes a fire port in the kiln after tossing rock salt into the propane-fueled blaze. The salt vaporizes at the 2,300° temperature and fuses with silica in the clay to form a hard, corrosion-resistant glaze with a characteristic "orange-peel" texture.

OVERLEAF: NATIONAL GEOGRAPHIC PHOTOGRAPHER OTIS IMBODEN

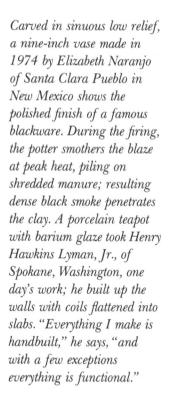

Carved in sinuous low relief, a nine-inch vase made in 1974 by Elizabeth Naranjo of Santa Clara Pueblo in New Mexico shows the polished finish of a famous blackware. During the firing, the potter smothers the blaze at peak heat, piling on shredded manure; resulting dense black smoke penetrates the clay. A porcelain teapot with barium glaze took Henry Hawkins Lyman, Jr., of Spokane, Washington, one day's work; he built up the walls with coils flattened into slabs. "Everything I make is handbuilt," he says, "and with a few exceptions everything is functional."

85

Plunging iron into a bed of coals, 80-year-old blacksmith Stewart Fahnstrom heats the metal to a malleable state before forging it into a boot-scraper at the restored Swedish town of Bishop Hill, Illinois. With 65 years of experience, he appraises a red-hot piece of metal. From a few original fragments, he created ironwork in the chandelier above — one of five — for the old church at Bishop Hill.

His custom jobs include a trunk lock of an old Swedish type. "I took up the trade because I had a strong desire to do this work," he says. "Now I teach it, too."

Trainee pewterer Kevin Jenness opens a mold to reveal a spoon he has just cast at Old Sturbridge Village. A tin alloy hardened by copper or antimony or bismuth, pewter formed the basic tableware of many Americans until about 1800. Thereafter pewterers adopted a harder, shinier pewterlike metal called Britannia, used by the New York partners Boardman & Hart for the teapot at left. Tinsmith Albert Lees of Old Sturbridge carefully solders a lantern punctured to let candlelight shine through in an attractive pattern. The spreading tail of a zinc peacock marked the shop of a Connecticut tinsmith in the early 19th century. A hand-painted 175-year-old coffeepot from Connecticut shows the simple, utilitarian styling of most tinware, made from sheet iron dipped repeatedly in molten tin.

Reflecting changes in taste and style, the art of silversmithing has flourished in America for more than three centuries. A footed sugar box, made by John Coney of Boston in the late 1600's, shows the elaborate lines, curves, and high relief of the baroque style. In contrast, a New York teakettle (upper right) from about 1720 has simpler lines and more restrained decoration. In the 1750's ornamentation again became popular; a pear-shaped coffeepot by Philip Syng, Jr., of Philadelphia exemplifies the delicate scrolls, flowers, and leaves of rococo. Highly ornate factory ware of the mid-19th century provoked the arts and crafts movement, an effort to revive handwork and good design. In this spirit Robert R. Jarvie of Chicago —an admirer of Revere—adapted an 18th-century flagon for a pitcher, dated 1911. He added strapwork with a chasing hammer and deliberately left visible hammer marks as proof of handcraft. Contemporary silversmith Imogene Gieling of San Francisco cradles a container adorned with golden goats and ancient Roman glass. "I am striving," she says, "for forms . . . so much a part of the entire life process, that it is undetermined whether they are being built up or worn away."

Lusterless silver acquires the polished elegance of a sauceboat in the hands of journeyman silver-smith Jim Curtis at Williamsburg. Following inscribed lines, he cuts the body from sheet silver. With a compass he marks guidelines for symmetry. Hammering the metal on an oak block, he begins the shaping process. "Strokes with a raising hammer must be gentle and precise," he warns as he shapes the sides on an anvil. A wooden mallet straightens any distortions. On a leather sandbag, Curtis "sinks" the curvature of

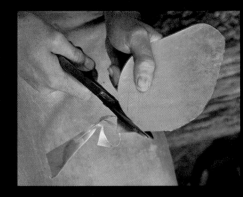

the bottom; then, on the block, that of the spout. "The talent of the silversmith—just like the sculptor's—shows in the shaping," he says. When hardened from hammering, the silver becomes malleable again with heating in a charcoal fire. Once Curtis has shaped the piece, he stamps the maker's mark and, with a flat-headed hammer, begins planishing—smoothing the surface by light taps. Using a chasing hammer, he sharpens decorative detail, then fits the cast feet. Filing produces a gracefully scalloped edge before Curtis fits the handle. A last thorough polishing with jeweler's rouge results in the brilliant sheen of the completed sauceboat.

DAVID HISER

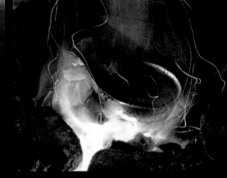

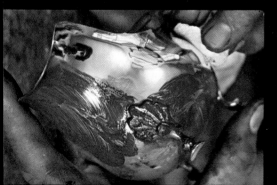

4

Fiber and Fabric

HIS HANDS MOVED SWIFTLY and steadily, building a design of color and texture, thread by thread. Taft Greer, a tall, quiet man with a weary, gentle face, sat before the old loom which, he explained, "My grandmother give to me, and her grandmother give to her."

A weaver-craftsman by trade, Taft Greer makes coverlets in patterns handed down from generation to generation.

"It used to take six days to weave off a coverlet, but it takes me longer now that I don't have the use of myself like I used to."

Inside the gray walls of the weaving shed, I watched the taut white vertical threads of the warp slowly fill up and grow into the blocks and stripes of the Walls of Jericho pattern. I saw how, as Taft Greer's grandmother would say, "Weavin' makes the pretties come up."

First he pressed down on a treadle that raised two of the four harnesses hanging over the center of the loom. As they moved up, they lifted a series of warp threads above the others. Then, through the resulting open space, he threw the shuttle carrying red yarn. Next, he pulled the comblike batten forward to push the new row down evenly into place.

He worked without a "draft." He needed no paper pattern to show him which treadle to pump and which shuttle to throw.

Up and down went the harnesses. Left to right and back again slid the shuttles, sometimes the one wound with red, sometimes the one with white. Back and forth went the batten, its soft thud and the clatter of the treadles striking the only notes in the rhythm of the weaver, the sounds mingling with the quiet of the Tennessee hills.

There, high on a mountain slope in southern Appalachia, an American weaving tradition lingers on.

The "most ancient perhaps of all the arts of civilization"—so anthropologist Claude Lévi-Strauss describes weaving, which has a history covering thousands of years.

The closely related skills of basketry and mat-making are even older. The basic principles of weaving—of interlacing two sets of threads to form a web—are everywhere the same, but this process produces fabric as varied as taffeta and burlap.

In early America weavers produced plain cloth for daily needs: bed and table linens, blankets, sturdy fabrics for clothing. Dresses and shirts and trousers were often made of linsey-woolsey, a coarse material originally woven with a linen warp and a wool weft; it combined the warmth of wool and the strength of linen. Cotton and linen could be combined in the same way.

"But the woven coverlet is probably the most widely known product of the 18th- and 19th-century American handweaver," says Rita J. Adrosko, youthful curator in the Division of Textiles at the Smithsonian Institution in Washington, D. C. "These warm, washable, richly colored coverlets brightened interiors that might otherwise have been rather drab."

American weavers, I learned, did not create finery for the gentry. The prosperous merchants of the north and the plantation owners of the south imported fashionable fabrics from Europe. On May 27, 1746, a Boston newspaper advertised "*a great Variety*" from London: "India Dimetys . . . silk Damask . . . Velvet . . . worsted Stuff plain and flower'd . . . Broad Cloths, Serges . . . Chinces, Callicoes. . . ."

"Although American weavers supplied the wealthy with some household textiles, the colonial craftsman wove a greater variety of textiles for less affluent families," Rita Adrosko told me as we examined coverlets in the museum's collection.

I could see immediately how these fabrics— white with reds, or blues, or yellows, or warm browns—would enliven a house or cabin where luxuries were few. These were even prettier than I expected.

"Settlers brought the simple geometric coverlet designs from their homelands in Germany, Scotland, and other countries," said

BY CYNTHIA RUSS RAMSAY

Fingers still nimble at 88, Tildy Peck of Campton, Kentucky, quilts Grandmother's Flower Garden—an abstraction in cotton from discarded aprons and similar goods. Stitching from sunup to sunset, she pieces a quilt-top in one month; her Postage Stamp pattern takes as many as 4,000 scraps. Developed as functional items for specific needs, American fiberwork and design have survived the Machine Age to emerge as distinctive handcrafts and vigorous forms of folk art—or innovation.

Rita. "Contrary to popular belief, coverlet weaving was not born in America."

"Who made these coverlets?" I asked.

"Some were woven by home weavers, and some were the work of professionals. Most housewives, even if they knew how to weave, made plainer cloth. But some housewives skilled enough to produce coverlets exchanged drafts—weaving patterns—in the same way that women exchange recipes today.

"Spinning wheels were much more common than looms," Rita added, turning to her files for some statistics. "The 1810 census in a county in Pennsylvania counted 9,989 spinning wheels in use and 325 looms in a total population of 29,703. Many more people were involved in spinning than in weaving. After all, it takes a great deal of yarn to supply a weaver."

I had read about the itinerant weavers who went from town to town, from settlement to settlement, carrying their pattern books with them. And Taft Greer had told me how his grandmother, born in 1833, "would go and stay with folks for a week, two weeks at a time and weave for 'em. She wove hundreds and hundreds of bedspreads. That's all she know'd what to do."

The designs had fanciful names like Indian March, Sea Star, Noah's Wonder, Philadelphia Pavement, and Bonaparte's Retreat.

"There're *hundreds* of patterns," said Persis Grayson, seated by a spinning wheel in the bright, modern living room of her home in Kingsport, Tennessee. "But there are many more names.

"In one area the pattern St. Anne's Robe became Governor's Garden. In others it was Beauty of Kaintuck and Rocky Mountain Cucumber. It also appears as Susan Lindsay's Draft, Christian Ring, and Poken Dalis—for President James K. Polk and Vice President George M. Dallas."

For the first two hundred years of America's history women and children in practically every household knew how to card and spin. Now Persis Grayson—teacher, lecturer, weaver, with silver hair and a stunning smile—travels to craft schools, workshops, and universities to revive the nearly forgotten art of spinning by hand.

My sons Andrew, age nine, and David, eleven, decided to take a turn at the traditional child's chore of carding. "It's fun," concluded Andrew, "but it sure would get boring if I had to do it all the time."

While the boys quickly learned to comb wool between two wire-studded wooden paddles, called cards, I struggled with the spinning wheel. I tried to draw the fleece so it would twist into thread evenly, without breaking or bunching up into rough spots and nubs. Like many things that look easy, spinning takes skill.

It also takes strong legs. Persis told me that a woman might walk as far as 12 miles in an ordinary day's work of spinning wool—three feet back as she turned the wheel and drew the wool out, three feet forward to wind the thread on the bobbin.

To spin flax, women used a smaller "low" wheel turned by a foot pedal. That seems easier, but flax takes many long, hard hours to prepare. I was amazed to learn how difficult it was to separate the fine linen fiber from the tough core and outer sheathing.

The flax is "retted" in water to rot the stems partially. Then, when the stalks have dried out thoroughly, a flax brake pounds them, scutching knives scrape them, and "hetchels" or "hackles" comb and separate the long, fine fiber from the short tow.

In an account of life in the southern highlands in the 19th century, Rebecca Dougherty Hyatt records just how you get flax for "menfolks Sunday-meetin' clothes, table kivers, an' bed sheets."

You "sow hit on Good Friday an' pull hit the first of August, an' sow hit thick as hair on a hog's back.... If hit ain't rotted sufficient and if you ain't keerful with yer scutchin' an' hacklin' hit wastes a sight bad...."

As for the tow: "You weave hit in wagon kivers an' bed tickin' an' other rough stuff. Hit's best to bile the tow thread out good in a pot o' ashes to saften hit up and break the stiff out'n hit afore hit's wove."

"It's hard to understand how these women got everything done," said Persis. I was thinking the same thing.

Persis showed me a sample book thick with swatches of cloth woven in mountain homes nearly a century ago: page after page pinned with pieces of linsey and jeans (a twilled cotton) in vibrant purples, blues, and reds.

"Most of the time we see the old cloth after it has been faded by hundreds of washings. This is what the colors were really like," said Persis, turning to a deep, lustrous blue pinstriped with rosy red.

"It's the use of color which expresses the mountain woman's yearning for beauty. She created beauty with color in the quilts she designed, the rugs she braided, and the yarn she dyed for her weavings."

The many tones of blue in early American textiles came from the indigo plant. The bright reds came from madder root or from cochineal, the dried and ground-up bodies of a female insect native to Mexico and lands farther south. Pack peddlers carried the lumps of indigo and the packets of cochineal and madder from door to door.

But for most of her colors the mountain woman and the early American housewife concocted dyes from plants in the forest or in her garden. These women knew how to boil blossoms, leaves, roots, berries, and bark to bring out the color.

Each batch allowed a woman to experiment: a few grains of copperas to make walnut dye darker, a pinch of alum to turn hickory bark a greenish yellow. Generally, she followed recipes—like the one for Rebel gray remembered by Rebecca Dougherty Hyatt.

"You gather yer sourwood leaves, a right smart chance o' them, and put a layer in yer big iron wash pot, then a layer o' clean washed wool," it begins. You let the mixture stand "nine days, or 'til hits sour'd and riz up. Then build yer fire right under, but bring hit to a slow bile. . . ." Cooked three or four hours, the wool turns "blacker than a witch's cat."

Three pounds of black wool to one of white, picked and carded together before spinning, give you a Confederate homespun "the color of gray the reg'lar sol'jers wore."

Not until Mary Frances Davidson, a pioneer in preserving the craft of the dye pot, emptied a large bag of yarn onto her sofa did I realize the range and vibrance of vegetable-dyed colors. The tumble of small hanks in tones of gold, green, purple, pink, and beige offered a feast for the eyes.

"When I first saw the beauty and harmony of the natural dyes," she told me, "I realized I was color hungry. I was teaching math at a high school in Oak Ridge then, but I knew I wanted to make a living at this."

She has; and now thick skeins of yarn, buckets and tubs, and jars filled with powders crowd the side porch of her home outside Gatlinburg, Tennessee. The white sink in the kitchen changes its stains from day to day.

Josie Higgins, a petite woman with delicate features, has a harder time—she makes quilts for a living. One quilt takes her two weeks and costs her $10 for material: pieces of print fabric, lining, and polyester batting. She works

Natural dyes color a hooked rug made about 1838 for a New England floor. Such homemade rugs, native to North America, long remained popular in rural areas. Woven in wool and embroidered with woolen yarn in 1778, a heavy bed covering from Connecticut shut out winter chill by night and brightened the room by day with its browns made from butternut and its now-faded blue.

for a craft guild that pays her $48 for a product that brings nearly $100 in city shops.

Josie was piecing a quilt top on a 1902 sewing machine when I saw her in Spruce Pine, a town in the North Carolina mountains. She sewed diamond-shaped patches together into squares with a star pattern. Stripes, gingham checks, flowers, figures combined into a design that escaped garishness by sheer artistry.

With all the squares sewed together, the actual quilting would begin. Josie would set up the quilting frame, stretch the backing over it, lay the batting on it, and stretch the pieced cover on top, pulling all three layers over the wooden rack, good and tight. Then, with tiny, even hand stitches, Josie would follow the lines of the star and quilt the layers together, the way she has been doing for about 65 years.

"The first I ever done was on my grandma's quilt. I couldn't see up over the frame, so they set me up on a nail keg, and they gave me a needle and thimble. Hit wasn't any good, but they bragged on it."

Josie remembers an earlier time, when people needed quilts to keep warm, when thrifty housewives were loath to throw away bits of cloth. She remembers when folks would come in wagons from miles around for a quiltin'.

Amish women still gather around the quilting frame, especially in the fall when they've finished their canning, cooked the apple butter, dried the corn. Cora Schrock invited me to a quilting on her farm in a remote corner of western Maryland.

"Welcome to the stitch and blabber club," said a sweet-faced woman as we were introduced. But the talk of the occasion, sometimes in English, sometimes in a lilting German dialect, was sporadic and leisurely. The talk of intimate friends.

Eighteen quilters sat on four benches around the frame. They bent over their work, their hair pulled back under stiff net caps—white for married women, black for girls. They rarely looked up. Needles darted in and out, following a scroll design chalked on the plain blue border.

"The fine, tiny stitches make the design fluff up," Cora pointed out to me before calling us to a splendid lunch—"food, after all, is part of every quilting."

The technique of quilting originated many centuries ago; it was practiced in ancient China and in ancient Egypt; it spread from Europe to the colonies as a matter of course.

"But only in America did quilt-making trigger such an explosion of extraordinary abstract design," says Jonathan Holstein, a collector of quilts, an authority, an enthusiast.

"Certainly quilts can be masterpieces of craft," he points out, "but we see the overall designs before the stitches." He and his wife, Gail van der Hoof, have collected hundreds, rescuing quilts used as painters' dropcloths, as padding in antique shipments, as ground cover at flea markets.

"As the 19th century began," he says, "American women were forming the design trends that later quilters took to such heights and used in such quantity.

"Appliqué was for 'best' quilts; the pieced quilt was for everyday. Both types are sometimes called patchwork.

"Designs spread as women borrowed ideas from each other and took patterns with them when families moved. Reputations rose and fell with the beauty of the quilts and the skill with which they were worked."

Women of every class quilted. This was one form of needlework that leisured ladies and overburdened housewives learned to do.

Young girls, of course, recorded their repertoire of embroidery on their samplers. At age five or six, a little girl was ready to learn to sew and learn to read; her finished sampler was its own diploma, duly hung on the wall for all to see.

Fashionable schools in the 18th century taught young ladies many kinds of stitchery. A notice in the *Boston News-Letter* from August 1716 offers lessons in "Quilting...all sorts of fine Works, as Feather-Work, Filegre... Embroidering a new way, Turkey-Work for Handkerchiefs..., fine new Fashion Purses, flourishing and plain Work...."

Thomas Jefferson, in a letter to his 14-year-old daughter Martha, advises her not to neglect her needlework: "In dull company, and in dull weather, for instance, it is ill-manners to read, it is ill-manners to leave them.... The needle is then a valuable resource. Besides, without knowing how to use it herself, how can the mistress of a family direct the work of her servants?"

Bertha Cook learned knotting and hand-tied fringing for another reason.

It was almost dusk, and mist veiled the Blue Ridge when I arrived at Mrs. Cook's home in Boone, North Carolina.

"Anything folks had, they had to make themselves. It took a lot of work, but that's the way it was," she said.

With practiced hands she wound the white thread into a round neat knot and fastened it to the white cotton bedspread with a quick jab of the needle. Again and again. In time, thousands of thread beads would trace the grape and vine pattern on the spread, a design of white on white.

"My mother, aunts, and grandmothers all knew how to do colonial knotting. They made it for their own homes, for bedspreads and curtains. My mother kind of pinched down on me to make sure I learned to knot and tie fringe. Now I've made something over a thousand spreads, and I have more orders from folks at the crafts fair than I can fill."

Margaret Haass Clark, who lives near Washington, D. C., a matron with a tweedy elegance and an easy charm, took up needlepoint for yet another motive.

"My oldest child was learning to drive a car, and I had to keep busy to keep from worrying myself sick. I turned to needlepoint because the wools are so pretty. I would sit in the front seat with my eyes on that canvas!

"Anybody can do needlepoint—and I am anybody! I've also found that needlework allows me to express my feelings in an interesting, personal way. I have a friend who helps me work out the designs."

The cushions, upholstery, rugs, and wall hangings in her modern home overlooking the Potomac River offer something store-bought, mass-produced textiles can never do. They are whimsical, imaginative, decorative pieces that meet her needs and reflect her ideas and taste perfectly.

"And they had been," she said, "fun to make and a pleasure to use."

Like countless individuals in America's past, Margaret Clark has brought beauty into her home. Like Taft Greer and Josie Higgins, Persis Grayson and Bertha Cook, she has worked long and hard to master the techniques of her craft. In the process she developed an informed respect for sound workmanship and she grew familiar with fabrics rich in color, pleasing in design.

I have learned that American textiles had a charm and beauty born in surroundings where craftsmen had to spin and weave and stitch to keep their families clothed and warm. But perhaps my most heartening discovery is this: that with a rich heritage to nurture a sense of style and with a willingness to learn the skills of needle or loom, almost anyone can create beauty—who truly wants to.

"It takes a lot of work, and there's a knack to it, too," says Mrs. Bertha Cook of Boone, North Carolina, as she stitches hundreds of tiny knots on a spread. With a darning needle and a shuttle she ties thread into fringe, or netting, for a bed canopy. In this detail of an 1820's coverlet, relief fixed by intricate needlework marks the trapunto style of quilting.

On a hand loom from 1801, Tennessee craftsman
Taft Greer weaves a coverlet in the Walls of Jericho
pattern (with shuttle, below). Pine Tree motif
borders a double-weave Lover's Knot bedspread
with cotton warp (vertical) and woolen weft (hori-
zontal). Plaid homespun survived hard wear on a
Utah sheep farm in pioneer days. A 19th-century
print suggests a self-reliant family: father weaving,
mother spinning, a son starting a mat of rushes,
little brother working—or playing—with a mallet.

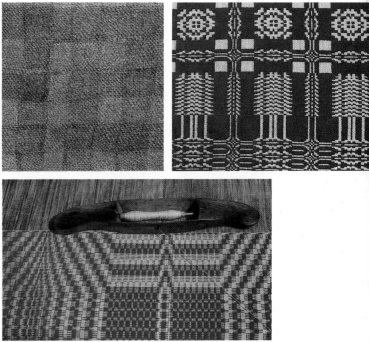

LOWELL GEORGIA (OPPOSITE AND DETAIL ABOVE)

Blankets and rugs of expert craftsmanship have won Navajo women wide recognition as weavers in the past century. Here neighbors demonstrate weaving at the Hubbell Trading Post in Ganado, Arizona—a bartering center since 1876. Working at home, where they still produce almost all of their rugs, they can set up the vertical looms between trees. Sheep from the reservation supply the wool Mary Begay (left) spins into yarn. Navajos learned weaving from men of the Pueblo tribes in the 18th century and soon developed patterns of their own. Encouraged by traders like J. Lorenzo Hubbell, the Post's founder, who supplied them with synthetic aniline dyes, they began making thicker and heavier blankets that appealed to white purchasers as rugs. Hubbell especially favored rich "Ganado red" rugs like that at lower left. The so-called "Chief's blanket" evolved over the years as one of the finest examples of a changing style; the one shown at left center dates from about 1882, in the period of highest development.

"It takes magic in the fingertips," says Cherokee basket-
maker Lottie Stamper, weaving
a basket base with hard-to-
work river cane. First taught
by her mother, she revived
the nearly lost and intricate
technique of double weaving
after studying museum photographs; here a finished single
weave sits next to a smaller
though stronger double weave.
Nova Scotia's Micmac Indians
make tiny twined-grass-and-
wood baskets for gifts (below).

LOWELL GEORGIA

Triangle-decorated California Maidu basket, two inches high, once held trinkets or jewelry.
The Panamint basket from Death Valley, of coils sewn together with cactus-spine awls, served
a similar purpose. A Paiute decoy, of skin glued on tule stems, simplified duck hunting.

Makah Indians of the Pacific Northwest still fashion sturdy baskets by the method called wrapped twining—wrapping a tough grass around cedar roots or bark strips. Made about 1900 for sale as novelties, three miniature covered containers show the technique. An unknown woman wove the basket at far right on a glass jar.

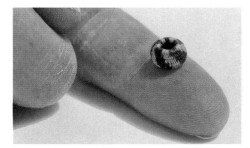

One of the world's smallest, a coiled-weave Pomo basket proclaims the artist's virtuosity. Only a quarter-inch in diameter, it resembles a larger version, much easier to make. Living on the central California coast, Pomo women excelled in coiled-weave techniques used by tribes to the southward and in twined-weave basketry similar to that of northwestern neighbors. They still employ their full range of skills. Shells complement black quail feathers and yellow meadowlark plumage on a Pomo basket for ceremonial use. "Basketry is the mother of all loom work and beadwork," wrote specialist Otis T. Mason in 1902. "The first and most versatile shuttles were women's fingers."

*White-oak ribs bend into shape around a wooden mold as José
F. Reyes begins a Nantucket lightship basket in his island shop.
Rattan, imported from the Orient, hangs ready for weaving
when the ribs set. Crews manning the lightship at the treacherous
Nantucket Shoals first wove the baskets more than a century ago,
to pass the lonely hours. Scholars debate the origin of this sturdy,
wooden-bottomed design, but it appears certain that seamen
returning from Pacific waters introduced rattan. Modern craftsmen employ the original techniques; little differentiates time-
darkened open baskets (below), made 100 years ago, from newer
models. Ivory-topped covers have helped the baskets win prestige
as summer handbags. Graduated sets of molds, designed by the
lightship men, made it easy to produce "nests" of baskets;
these allowed convenient storage of the household carry-alls.*

NATIONAL GEOGRAPHIC PHOTOGRAPHER BATES LITTLEHALES

107

Fascinated by novel sheen and color, Indians traded fine furs for glass beads. At right, beadwork embellishes a Comanche pipe pouch 28 inches long and covers a rare Klamath basket nearly 4 inches high. Often, as beads became available, new designs replaced the ancient geometric motifs of porcupine quillwork. Indian women near the Great Lakes learned curved and floral patterns in French mission schools, and the art spread westward. In the 1880's, it seems, a Crow wife inadvertently inverted the Stars and Stripes on a gauntlet for her husband, an Army scout. The Crows developed high skill with floral motifs, as in the detail from a horse's breastplate. Alien culture increasingly influenced Indian art. By about 1900, only beading technique and cradleboard remain

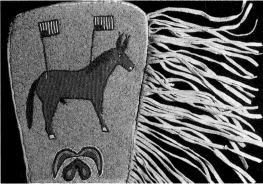

recognizably Indian in a Chippewa toy—complete with imported velvet bands and a bisque "Florodora" doll manufactured in Germany.

ABC's of needlework: Samplers taught girls of early America lessons considered necessary for good wives. While perfecting a variety of stitches, girls sewed moral precepts or verses of Scripture into their designs. Samplers figured among the few prized possessions settlers brought from Europe, and have ranked as treasured heirlooms in American families from the earliest decades to the present.

Sampler-learned stitches slip into place in a pastoral scene embroidered by a young woman who may have composed verse and certainly chose a poem to suit her picture. Formerly needlework offered women one of the few trades open to them; it still provides enjoyment. A New England chair cover from about 1730 inspires Dorothy Littlehales's crewel, or embroidery in wool.

Needlepoint, past and present: Dressed as colonial gentlefolk, Adam and Eve appear among the creatures of Eden—rendered in petit-point tent stitch, wool on linen. This Biblical idyll comes from the hands of a New England lady who had leisure enough for such devout and decorative work. A border patterned on camera film frames a needlepoint biography of photographer Edward Clark, a project that took his wife, Margaret, five years. "I used symbols to represent highlights of Ed's life and career, including World War II," explains Mrs. Clark, of Bethesda, Maryland. "For example, the postmarks at the upper left record the civil rights struggles Ed covered; the chevrons and white rose of York recall the Sergeant York story that got Ed his job with Life magazine in 1941; the two trees beside the Clark house stand for his sons and their families."

*"Crocheting is perhaps the most versatile
of all needlework,"* says Cindy Picchi of
New York City, *who adapts its stitches
to items as varied as fantasy animals,
wall hangings, and contemporary coats.
She made the version at left with homespun wool, using goldenrod for mustard-
color dye. She embroidered the wool-
on-Pelon lining and appliquéd it with
velvet. "Crochet is three-dimensional,"
Cindy feels, "lending itself to free design
and to an almost unlimited spectrum of
materials and techniques." Working with
wool, rope, metallics, linen, and many
other flexible materials, she creates her
avant-garde sculpture. She likes "being
unconfined, able to build up and out as
well as long and wide." Her "Seabeast"
stands three feet long and two feet high.
Intricate as many crochet designs appear,*

DAVID DOUBILET

*all involve the simple hook and a wrapping
of yarn or thread—as Cindy uses them
to complete a coat hem (above). One
hundred years ago Rita Hageman, of
South Branch, New Jersey, employed them
to edge a linen doily with iris blossoms.*

Varied blocks, no two identical, define the album quilt, extremely popular in 19th-century Baltimore; Mary Everist made this fine specimen about 1850. Usually, close friends and relatives worked and signed one square apiece to make a quilt intended as a present, giving the type an alternate name, "friendship quilt." Below, a square-rigged ship in crewel and appliqué —also from Baltimore—exemplifies the intricate detail and sure workmanship of the tradition. During the 1800's quilting bees became an American passion. In a single winter a housewife might take part in 25 to 30 quilting sessions, some four days long. Young girls would piece quilt tops for their hope chests, and only after a formal engagement would they under-take the actual quilting. An old saying warned: "If a girl has not made a quilt by her 21st year, no man will want to marry her." Sometimes, the story goes, girls still single would gently toss a cat on a finished quilt—when the cat managed to jump off, the maiden closest to the spot would be the next to marry.

"Sewing I learned from my grandmother," says Mrs. Charles Short of Wolf Summit, West Virginia. "Now I make my nine grandchildren clothes they wouldn't get no other way." Wearing a homemade "mutton-sleeved" dress, she hands on her knowledge of "knotting" or tying a comforter to Joyce Miller at Salem College's Heritage Arts Center. A toy from the 1850's sets hickory-nut-headed dolls at a quilting frame. In a unique collage of scraps, pieced but never quilted, a crazy-quilt-to-be commemorates boxer John L. Sullivan, surrounded by embroidered headlines from Chicago newspapers. The crazy quilt made striking use of waste materials, but Victorian needlewomen often incorporated expensive fabrics—velvets, brocades, figured silks, glossy satins—and added fancy embroidery and spangles as well.

LOWELL GEORGIA

Diamonds of color create the Broken Star, one of many popular star motifs, in this pieced quilt from Panhandle, Texas. The work of Frances Knight Silcott in 1939, it reflects the artistry required to fit fragments of fabric into a complex design. Calico and black shape a Monkey Wrench quilt by Ora Watson of Deep Gap, North Carolina; she calls her Log Cabin quilt (lower right) "real hard to make because the pieces are so little."

Square blocks in sawtooth rows carry out the pattern called Sunshine and Shadow for a quilt stitched in Pennsylvania sometime between 1880 and 1910. It shows the Amish preference for solid colors in vibrant combinations; apparently sunlight has faded two of the borders. Painstaking needlework shapes the curved lines of Field Daisy, sewn by Tildy Peck, and Double Wedding Ring, by Bonnie Steelman, Mrs. Watson's niece.

Sun and starfish on the island of Cyprus inspired Arlinka Blair's wall hanging; she stood on linoleum block

to print the designs by her own weight. Hand cording binds the three printed squares to the backing.

Pulling her thread taut, Swedish-born Ragnhild Langlet works on "Spacescape," an abstraction on two adjoining linen circles with embroidery and appliqué of mica. "Mysterious Cache from Tomb #55" aptly titles Katherine Westphal's wall hanging; it conveys impressions of Egypt. Her quilt "The Hunt" captures figures from a 16th-century French tapestry. Both works combine batik and quilting. The mummy's face represents loom-woven tapestry, stitched to the batik; and free-hanging yarns of the warp become the tresses.

5

In the Mountains

IN HIS 97TH YEAR, Preston Blair no longer uses his finest creation, except to stir warm memories. We sat on the porch of his home on Blair Ridge Road, near Bradleyville, Missouri, and I watched his fingers run lovingly over the banjo his son Everett handed him.

Once Preston cared so much about music that he worked for many weeks in the only way he knew to own a good instrument. He made it himself. Save for the hardware bought from a mail order catalogue, and calfskin covering for the hoop, Preston made his banjo from scratch in 1906, felling trees for the various woods.

He had no pattern, but he had seen other banjos. His experience lay in making a couple of crude small models, virtual toys by comparison. His tools and skills were those he had been using and acquiring by necessity as he entered young manhood on a rocky mountainside farm.

A slip of a 12-year-old boy, he reached his new home in Taney County back in 1890. The last great wave of more than 60 years' migration from the Appalachians to the Ozarks had brought his family here from Letcher County, Kentucky. They came as homesteaders, to settle on new land. Like other migrants from the east, they came schooled in the realities of life in the hills—a self-sufficiency based on the philosophy of make-do, do-for-yourself, or do without.

Throughout the Ozarks, descendants follow the precepts of their forefathers. They may use a truck instead of a horse-drawn sled and their wives and daughters may quilt under fluorescent lights, but they remain masters of improvising and "getting by."

Preston and Everett Blair raise and preserve much of their own food, use tools and furniture Preston made years ago. They showed me a chair with a woven hickory-bark seat, and Preston patiently explained how the posts were shaped green and joined with well-seasoned rungs. Fitted together, the drying posts would shrink and grip the rungs more firmly than today's best glue could hold them.

But the banjo captured my fancy. The neck is rich red cedar, shaped and sanded with precision, inlaid with lighter woods and a photograph of the young maker. The hoop is amazing: a circle of unvarying thickness, from one strip of hard-to-bend elm. Young Preston had painstakingly feathered each end of the strip. After gluing the ends, he had burnished the seam so smooth I could detect it only by eye, not by touch. And untold hours of work had assured a good true sound.

Did Preston consider himself a craftsman? "Oh, no," he chuckled.

Later, Everett explained his father's answer and what the word "craftsman" implies to him: "To him, his work is part of our way of life, not an art. What he made was for a specific use or, like the banjo, for his own pleasure."

Preston has made plenty of things in his time, and done plenty of hard work. When he bought the house he lives in now, back in 1929, its source of water was a spring a quarter of a mile away, some 150 feet lower in elevation. He bought a pumping device called a hydraulic ram and installed it himself, laying the pipe. Everett still recalls the cheers when the first drops of water appeared at the house.

I had seen a photograph of the house in which Preston Blair was born, and decided I must go back to Appalachia to see if I could find traces of the heritage by which this unusual man had lived. He remembered the place as a short distance up a tributary of Rockhouse Creek near Jeremiah, Kentucky. The little town still appeared on most road maps, but beyond that I was not optimistic.

With my friend Larry Price at the controls of his small plane, we tipped a wing in salute above Preston's hilltop home and in less than five hours we were in Hazard, Kentucky. The next morning we set out in a rented car. We turned off one highway onto another, took a pinched little road up a mountain hollow by a

BY CLAY ANDERSON

PHOTOGRAPHED BY LOWELL GEORGIA

stream called Blair Branch. Roughly half the mailboxes bore the surname Blair—promising evidence, but almost too much.

Finally I repeated my story to Arlie Adams, in whose driveway we found a place to turn. Abruptly he said, "Maybe Dee can help," and we walked over to the neat board-and-batten house of his brother-in-law.

Dee Blair indeed could help. He knew some Blairs who had visited Preston in Missouri. He studied the homeplace photo I had borrowed, then boomed in sonorous tones, "Why yes. That's my father's house." And when I mentioned Preston's banjo, Dee's wife ducked into the house and returned to hand me something: another homemade banjo.

In this one the neck was red oak, without inlay, and less hardware had been used to cover the hoop—with groundhog hide. In fact, it had been bought from a neighbor and relative also named Preston Blair, dead several years. All these Blairs are cousins, of course, and brothers when it comes to making music. "There was a while the boys got together and played music a right smart. We still have her here," acknowledged Dee.

"I hear him playing over here ever oncet in a while," added Arlie.

At 53, Dee Blair is a gentle bear of a man, obviously not so powerful as in his youth but not softened by disability. I could imagine him and my friend Preston as brothers a century ago. I began to question him about the craft skills of which I saw evidence.

"I was pretty good until I got hurt," Dee explained. "Done about a little of everything." His years of work in the coal mines and with a railroad section gang had ended with an accident and a period of illness.

When he felt least able, Dee Blair probably did the most historically significant work of his lifetime. He passed the hours whittling and crafting miniatures of objects he knew as a boy—a log cabin, a tiny coffin, a plow, a yoke, a water trough and a rain barrel like the ones

Ozark mountaineer Preston Blair, approaching his centennial year, cradles a banjo he made in 1906; a photograph inlaid in its neck shows him as a young man. Like thousands of Eastern mountaineers before them, Preston and his parents moved to the Ozarks late in the 19th century, bringing from Kentucky their traditions of independence and hardiness, self-reliance and self-sufficiency.

his grandfather had hewed from a single log. He had a maul and a froe, its handle properly at right angles to the wedge-shaped blade for cleaving wood. He had made the metal parts from nails.

He had even built a model of the deceased Preston's ingenious contraption for getting water: a long fulcrum arrangement, delicately balanced with a kettle full of rocks, enabling one to lift a filled bucket from a well with a minimum of effort.

Dee Blair doesn't really consider himself a craftsman either. He has an anvil and forge. He picked up blacksmithing from Arlie's grandfather, but uses it mostly to make, repair, or sharpen tools for himself and his neighbors. He and Arlie work together butchering hogs. They grow garden truck in patches of land along the creek, as well as corn for the hogs and chickens and a pony, successor to the draft horses Dee has used all his life.

Dee doesn't take the pony up to cultivate the steep hillsides as he took the horses when he was younger, but he remains loyal to the old "bull tongue" plow which may very well have been invented for such conditions. That type of plow, named for the shape of the moldboard, stirred the soil instead of turning it, and was less likely to start erosion, hang up on roots, and bring rocks to the surface.

It doesn't "kill the soil," explained Dee, and the productivity of his patches bears him out. He told me just how he constructed the foot and beam of his plow from oak, with handles shaped from the limbs of a fallen but still living sourwood tree. He took me through his barn and shed to see tools he has made. "That's kinda what it takes to get by," he said.

And I knew I had found something I was looking for: a living link in a chain of craft tradition, an Appalachian counterpart to something I know in the Ozark hills.

I've been seeing Rex Harral at craft fairs in the Ozarks for nearly a decade, and he never fails to come up with some pioneer skill he wants me to record in words and pictures. Step by step we've gone through splitting rails, sharpening plowshares, making ax handles or corncob pipes, tanning leather.

I watched him one day at a fair in Forsyth, Missouri, while he worked on what looked like a foot-long split of stove wood. "My dad made these old spoons out of hickory," he told a circle of spectators.

Rex's skills with wood and metal parallel those of Dee Blair, and he came by them just

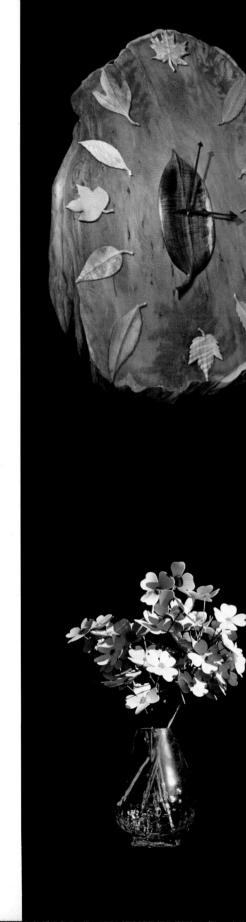

Appalachian craftsmen find inspiration around them: An owl in buckeye wood comes from the North Carolina studio of Cherokee woodcarver Virgil Ledford. Hazel Miracle, a Kentuckian, fashions dogwood blossoms with maple shavings from furniture that her husband and son make. Sawdust, glued and painted, forms the centers. North Carolinian Edd Presnell built the clock from a cedar burl; instead of numbers, he used 12 native woods, carving each to represent a leaf from that tree.

ACTUAL SIZES: OWL, HEIGHT 11½ INCHES; CLOCK, WIDTH 4 FEET; DOGWOOD, LIFE SIZE.

as informally. Rex's father was a blacksmith, carpenter, and farmer, and so is Rex.

But Rex has made a working farm into a tourist attraction of Wilburn, Arkansas, where he demonstrates his skills and sells his products. He also sells aprons, bonnets, pillows, and quilts made by his wife. In short, his approach to getting by extends into marketing. His wood turnings and wrought-iron work approach the status of art, and he is a fountain of new ideas of what will sell to tourists.

For all the things Rex Harral has going, I'm sure he won't mind my saying he doesn't make a lot of money. He's doing what it takes to get by, and doing it with a great deal of pride.

I watched him work with a block of hickory, the kind his father would start with when he needed an ax handle or a lard paddle. But Rex cuts his spoons with a gouge he made especially for this task and a favorite little drawknife. He duplicated the knife from a picture story on English chairmakers, and tempered it at his own forge. In half an hour he finished a spoon that probably would have taken his father a day's worth of leisure. And the two dozen spoons Rex sold in one day are likely more than his father made in a lifetime.

Producing for the tourist trade rather than for home consumption inevitably brings some changes, even in the most traditional crafts.

Elmer Kear spent the first 35 years of his life in the high country of eastern Tennessee. With the creation of Great Smoky Mountains National Park in 1926, he was forced to move from the home place. He settled just beyond the park boundary, in a narrow little hollow outside of Gatlinburg, with income prospects less than bright.

The family had grown a little broomcorn in the garden, and someone would assemble a few brooms for home use. In 1928, Elmer followed up a suggestion about supplementing his income. He laboriously assembled four dozen brooms in assorted sizes, loaded them on the back of an old mule, and took them to the shop of the Pi Beta Phi settlement school in Gatlinburg. The brooms sold—at prices ranging from 15 to 50 cents.

Over the next decade, Elmer gradually expanded his project—growing the broomcorn, splitting out handles from chestnut logs, gathering the poplar bark used as a binder. Finally broom-making was a full-time avocation (although Elmer continued to raise a garden and keep a cow). The life attracted Elmer's son, Omah, now 46, who has been working in the business since he was a teen-ager.

Omah runs the enterprise now, and while I watched him and his father assemble brooms —in what I assumed was the time-honored way—I asked if anything had changed since those first years.

"Everything nearly has changed," came the surprising reply.

True, no dyes have ever been used. The attractive reds and greens appear naturally, a prized aspect of broomcorn. But Omah described a variety of new developments. A commercial material has replaced poplar bark to bind the straw. A number of new tools have been devised. One strips the seed from an armful of broomcorn in a few seconds—it replaces Elmer's old method of drawing a single "sweep," or tuft, through a split fence-paling.

"If we hadn't improved," explained Omah, "we couldn't make a living." In the early years, Elmer made four different sizes and styles of brooms; Omah makes 30. These include many unusual handles, such as the spiral honeysuckle ones he buys in north Georgia, where his wife's people live.

The Kears grow two or three acres of broomcorn, but need the yield of 35 to 40 acres; they buy that, too.

Two of Omah's sons work at broom-making now; a third will finish school in 1976; still a fourth may join them. They produce more than 28,000 brooms a year, and Omah personally sorts and inspects every sweep of corn they use. They supply brooms to the Southern Highland Handicraft Guild, of which Elmer was a charter member, and have a waiting list of wholesale customers.

The best-selling Kear broom is still a curved-handle model Elmer began making in his earliest days as a craftsman. And his philosophy pretty much sets the pace for the entire operation: "If you put out sorry stuff, you'll ruin your trade."

A similar spirit marks the craft career of Jakey Grider of Highlandville, Missouri, who used hand skills to keep the hill farm his grandfather had bought. After service in the Korean war, he tried machine-shop work in industrial cities; he came home to try farming and bought his grandfather's place. When that fell short of supporting the family, he worked for a local firm, Native Wood Products Company, producing black-walnut wares.

In 1962, Jakey was in a car accident that

claimed the lives of his father and brother and left him with broken ribs, arms, and legs. As he convalesced, he turned to working with wood at home, making items like candle holders. Dust grew so thick in the house that his wife, Betty, finally insisted he build a shop.

Then, one day, he was out on the farm cutting some small locust trees. A look at the cross section of a fresh-cut tree inspired his new career. To Jakey the grain and color of that piece of locust looked just like a jewel.

Soon he was salvaging limbs and knots, sprouts and roots from nearly every tree that grows in the Ozarks: sassafras, dogwood, redbud, oak, hickory, buckeye, smoketree, sumac, ash, gum, pawpaw, persimmon, and many others. Cut and sanded and polished, these woods became an endless variety of necklaces, pendants, earrings, cuff links, and the like.

By 1970, with business growing rapidly, Jakey and Betty were earning a full-time living on the old home place; and they hope their four children will join in as they finish their schooling.

Even if Jakey Grider's work seems too original to belong to the heritage of traditional crafts, his delight in his medium surely is part of that heritage.

Moreover, consumer demand plays its part in the work of a woman who has made hundreds of cornshuck dolls—and shuck dolls must be practically as old as the culture of corn.

May Ritchie Deschamps of Swannanoa, North Carolina, fondly remembers the rag dolls she made and played with in the early years of this century, as oldest of 14 children of a family living in Viper, Kentucky. She first tried her hand at cornhusks about 43 years ago, to make a doll for her youngest daughter. Her husband, Leon Deschamps, was teaching surveying and drafting then at the John C. Campbell Folk School at Brasstown, North Carolina.

One day years later he was chatting with the manager of the Allanstand Shop in Asheville, who said she wished she knew *someone* to make shuck dolls. He said he thought May could manage it. May could.

She developed a technique for transforming damp shucks into charming figures with cornsilk hair. Before long, orders were coming in fast, and the demand shows no signs of abating. It takes three or four hours to make one doll—time varying with details of costume—so six of May's nine sisters and younger nieces and cousins help keep up the supply.

"I'm climbing 70 and never been in jail," says Willard Watson of Deep Gap, North Carolina. Ten years ago Willard began making intricately joined wooden toys that move: His mules walk, his chickens peck corn, and his farmers kick pigs.

Viper is only a few miles from Preston Blair's ancestral home, so I stopped in one evening to see the shuck dolls made by Mallie Ritchie and Kitty Ritchie Singleton. Their workshop is in the three-room house where their mother, Abigail Hall Ritchie, carded and spun wool and tended the 14 children. She took up weaving in 1934, worked at it until 1964, and—at May's urging—made rag rugs until she died in her 94th year.

I watched Mallie and Kitty making their beautiful playthings, and thought that there was really no equivalent for their occupation in early days of highland history—just harried mothers rapidly improvising plain dolls from the materials at hand. But who would rule out of the mountain tradition those cornshuck dolls made in the shadow of Abigail Hall Ritchie's now-silent loom?

Practically every significant factor in the craft heritage of the Appalachians seems to have a parallel in the Ozarks, with one possible exception. But this is an important one: the long-standing instruction at institutions like Berea College, the Hindman and Pine Mountain settlement schools in Kentucky; the Pi Beta Phi school in Gatlinburg; the Brasstown Folk School, and Miss Lucy Morgan's Penland School, in North Carolina. In 1930 these led in organizing the Southern Highland Handicraft Guild, now a highly efficient training and marketing group.

Photographer Lowell Georgia and I met one day on the still-secluded hilltop where the Penland School of Crafts was founded in 1929, and by happenstance our visit coincided with a visit by the founder.

A gambler's nerve and a missionary's zeal—both belied by her diminutive size and placid manner—enabled Lucy Morgan to persevere against odds that must have seemed overwhelming. Like many others who have fostered crafts in Appalachia, she had stressed weaving. She enjoys recounting how she and the Blue Ridge women weaving under Penland's auspices staked borrowed money and countless hours on a chancy prospect—that patrons of the Chicago World's Fair in 1933 would buy coverlets and scarfs from a tiny log cabin dwarfed by ostentatious exhibits. That effort was a great success.

In 1962, Miss Lucy turned over the direction of Penland to Bill Brown. He has followed her tough act both faithfully and well, but the interests of the mountain folks have changed.

Penland still teaches weaving, along with ceramics and woodwork and nine other courses, but most of the products would look more at home in a chic gallery than in a cabin up a hollow. And Penland, like Pi Beta Phi's Arrowmont School of Crafts in Gatlinburg, now attracts its students from all over the nation and from abroad as well.

On reflection, it occurred to me that such schools have adapted to meet contemporary needs—in the best traditions of the hill country. Craftwork has figured for decades in the programs of two colleges that ease their students' demands on family income.

Since 1906, the School of the Ozarks, at Point Lookout, Missouri, has accepted its students' required work as the equivalent of payment for tuition, room, and board.

Berea College, founded by abolitionists in 1855 to admit students regardless of color, continues to serve needy and deserving young people from Appalachia. It charges no tuition, but all students must work a minimum of ten hours per week. The average student earns about half the cost of room and board; extra work, with grants or loans, could pay it all. Prominent in this program is the school's craft industry: lapidary work, ceramics, woodworking (in which Dee Blair's son Marvon was enrolled), needlework, and home or "fireside" weaving.

These have strong links to the heritage of the mountains, but the products show a good deal more attention to marketability than most early settlers would have bothered with.

When the fireside weaving program began in the 1890's, one of those furnishing assistance was a shy little woman named Deborah Parsons. She had learned her craft from her mother, and used her knowledge in her native Estill County to warp looms for slave weavers. After her husband's death, new family arrangements put a six-year-old granddaughter under foot. Helena Barnett Cross remembers it this way:

"I dogged every footstep. I wound shuttles. I watched her warp. I'd hand her the threads —to where I think one day in self-defense to keep from killing me with a shuttle, she handed it to me and said, 'Do you want to try this?' And she made an excuse to walk away and leave me alone. I was in hog's heaven. I'd watched her so long, I knew how to weave."

Of Deborah Parsons's 69 grandchildren, Helena was the only one who learned to thread the loom and weave patterns. That was

47 years ago, and only 5 years ago did she get back to weaving on a serious and continuing basis—at a new home in Coal Hill, Arkansas.

I met Helena at the twenty-first Ozark Arts & Crafts Fair at War Eagle, Arkansas, held yearly on the third weekend of October. The fair attracts 100,000 people to a farm deep in the hills to inspect the work of more than 200 Ozarks artists and craftsmen. Sales reach nearly $50,000 a day. In short, the War Eagle fair is rivaled mainly by the Southern Highland Handicraft Guild's fairs in Gatlinburg in mid-October and in Asheville in mid-July.

Helena had enjoyed a success in Asheville, and found similar acceptance in the Ozarks. When I talked with her on the third day of the fair, she had just two items left in her booth. She showed me patterns she is heir to: Valley Forge Dogwood, Double Whig Rose, and her grandmother's favorite, Rose in the Wilderness. Deborah Parsons used the latter for a coverlet; Helena has reworked it as a matching rug, and even modified it as a shawl.

"Too many weavers never progress past crawling," says Helena. She stresses that she has never passed the learning stage in her profession. Of greater concern to her, her daughter has not been interested in learning to weave, and her three granddaughters live 700 miles away.

Such concerns weighed on my mind when I went to meet the Goodwin Weavers in Blowing Rock, North Carolina. John Goodwin represented at least the fourth generation of a weaving tradition extending all through the eastern mountains and back to England; he had died in July 1974, at the age of 85. He had no son.

John Goodwin's great-grandfather, John Owen Goodwin, reportedly had silk weavers on his estate in England in 1812. When his son James Cash was 21, the old man administered a whipping for something he misinterpreted as disobedience. James indignantly departed for America, survived a shipwreck, met his future wife on a rescue ship, and brought Goodwin weaving to Maryland, Virginia, and other parts of the New World.

The Goodwins—James Cash; his only son, Charles Eugene; and one of *his* sons, John— had what the family called "gypsy feet." They moved from one little water-powered weaving mill to another. They fled an outbreak of smallpox in Virginia, settled for a time in Tennessee, at Cumberland Gap. For a while Charles Eugene ran a mill in northern Georgia. His wife said she was careful not to get too attached to anything they couldn't haul in a wagon.

With a covered wagon the late John Goodwin began making his special contribution. He went out with "Uncle Bill" Walden, a bearded mountaineer, to travel through the Appalachians trading wool blankets and linsey material for raw wool. They would camp in an orchard, or other likely spot, and trade until time to move on.

Mountain women brought handwoven coverlets to show the traders, and John recorded them in drafts—"patterns" of dots or dashes or figures. His collection grew to several hundred; Lover's Knot, Whig Rose, Morning Star, and Honeycomb have become immensely popular since the Goodwins set up shop at Blowing Rock in 1951.

I learned all this from Mary Goodwin, whose own career was cut out for her by her father's passion for weaving. With time out for college, she has handled paper work and office details since she was 16.

Now the Goodwin Guild depends on an alliance between Mary and her sister's five children: Robert (Butch, to the family), Michael, who worked most closely with his grandfather, Margaret, John, and David.

A certified public accountant, David once undertook to improve the efficiency of Goodwin operations. As Margaret recalls, "It was impossible."

Butch, "the talker of the family," helped me understand why. The looms to which John Goodwin adapted his patterns are improved versions of those coming into use during the 1870's and '80's. The newest of the eight was in service by 1900. They work with a fine loud clatter, but the market offers nothing comparable today.

Mary recalls, "Daddy could step into the building and listen and know what loom was running, what loom was down, and what was wrong with it." I saw Butch do just that, restoring a balky loom to full, but less than lightninglike, speed. When parts are needed, Butch and Michael often have to make them or have them made. In short, the old looms are a CPA's nightmare. Butch says, "You kick 'em, cuss 'em, but you love 'em."

Customers love the products, prepared with a surprising amount of handwork for what is technically factory output: bedspreads, afghans, drapery materials, tablecloths. Some of the wholesale shops on the waiting list were buying from Mary Goodwin's grandfather, and everyone seems sure there will continue to be a Goodwin Guild.

In the Cornelison family, Robert (Buzz) would represent at least the fifth generation to work in the Bybee Pottery, at a Kentucky village of the same name, north of Berea. With his long hair, 27-year-old Buzz looks like a rock-and-roll musician. He is.

At age 18, his father, Walter, was totally involved in the pottery. At 46, Walter still spends his working day at his wheel in the log portion of the ramshackle pottery, talking with visitors who roam about at will.

I thought I heard disappointment in Walter's voice when he said Robert was "not particularly interested" in being a potter, and pride that his youngest son, Jimmy, is. Now 22, Jimmy had been entrusted with the job of overseeing the digging of the year's supply of clay. But Jimmy was off at college, and Buzz showed me around.

From the clay piled outside in the weather behind the building, to the finished ware rapidly disappearing from the shelves, Buzz gave me an inside look.

Mined from shallow veins in an open pit a couple of miles away, the clay is remarkably pure and requires no additives. When refined —cleaned of foreign substances like twigs or sand—it is crushed to powder and run through a pug mill, a bladed mixer that adds water. Fully prepared, the clay waits in a storage vault for the potter's wheel or the jigger wheel, a time-saving device for making shallow dishes. Ware shaped on the jigger wheel is formed with the help of plaster molds.

Walter Cornelison runs the potter's wheel; a veteran employee runs the jigger. Pieces that require handles or other additional work go to the finishing room. There two employees must judge the moment when pitchers, for example, are dry enough to hold a handle but not so dry that contrasting moisture in the clays will make a handle break off.

"We have our own palette of glazes, our own formulas, and they are secret," said Buzz. "It's fortunate that the process here at Bybee was always dip glazing. As far behind as we are on orders, dipping is fastest and most practical."

I asked about the empty shelves in the salesroom. "You got here too late. We open at 8 o'clock.

"It's wonderful. But you become so discouraged saying, 'Yes ma'am, but you'll have to wait eight weeks for that.' 'Why? I see some of them back there.' 'Yes, but you have 42 people ahead of you.'

"We're hoping to build another kiln. But you don't just advertise in the paper, 'Wanted: One Potter.' My father has done this all his life. He was reared on the wheel. I've been around it all my life, but I don't know the potter's wheel because I haven't spent that much time on it, and I've spent more time than the average college pottery student.

"I would hardly consider myself a potter in Daddy's shadow. He's phenomenal. . . .

"I'm the glib one," Buzz said in a self-deprecating way at one point, but he added that his father is a pretty good conversationalist, too, even at the wheel and not slackening a production pace. "Dad says he feels quite lonely over the wheel sometimes. After you've made 4,000 cream pitchers—you pretty well have the knack."

Buzz had a final insight: "Mother runs the shop. This is a matriarchy, and it always has been. Grandmother ran it. If you'll watch Mother, you'll see behind that smile there's a tiger. It's always been a good business. Mother has made it thrive."

When Dorothy Cornelison wrapped up the mugs and pots I was lucky enough to find, I utterly failed to see the tiger, but I thought of a question for Walter.

I got back to his wheel in time to hear him tell some visitors that a potter must have "the feel of clay. It's almost like it's alive. We'll say, 'It's working good today,' or 'I don't like this clay.' "

Then I asked him about prices. Didn't he think he could charge more, with supply lagging so far behind demand?

"Probably," he replied. "I may be stupid. We're trying to stay in a moderate price range. We're trying to make a practical pottery that people can afford to use and replace. Frankly, I hope we stay in business several more generations. I'm afraid some potters are going to price themselves out of the market."

Little of the craft work thriving in the highlands has as direct a line of descent as the Cornelisons'. Some reflects the activity of one enterprising man. The development of Ozarks woodcarving, for instance, has been fostered largely by Peter Engler and his two shops, in less than two decades. But over the same span of time, other craftsmen have seen their tradition fading.

Oscar Hensley of Saldee, Kentucky, runs

a sawmill and hires a cousin to go into the woods in summer to strip hickory bark for a chairmaking operation complete from stump to finished product. He made his first chair in the 1930's, using a shaving horse, and netted $1.50. Once there were 17 chairmakers in his vicinity, and now he's the only one left.

"The pay's gotten pretty good, too," remarked Oscar as he mused over a lack of interest from his sons and other young men he knows. "It takes patience," he conceded. "If you don't stick with it, you needn't to start."

"It took us ten years to get going to where we could even make a decent living," recalls Walter Woody. With his brother, Arval, he owns and operates a chair shop near Spruce Pine, North Carolina. And with any less tradition going for them, the Woody brothers might never have made it.

Arval showed me a yellowed newspaper clipping from the early 1930's, telling how his uncle Charlie and grandfather Arthur made walnut and maple chairs at a water-powered mill on Grassy Creek. "Uncle Art'er," as most everybody called him, had let the reporter know that he used to turn a chair in 30 minutes on a foot-powered lathe—as his father, Henry, and grandfather, Wyatt, might have done before him.

"Uncle Art'er" was well past 90, but still cutting an acre of grass with a scythe, when his grandsons revived the business after World War II, in a new concrete-block building with electrically powered equipment. He may have thought the boys were pretty soft.

Walter and Arval don't remember it as being all that easy. They assembled their ladderback straight chairs and rockers without glue by the old method and gave them an oil finish by hand rubbing. Occasionally they sold chairs from door to door in neighboring towns. When they made $3,000, as in the early 1950's, it was a big year.

Gradually, the world caught on to the sturdy chairs the brothers offer. Now they are six months behind on orders—all sales are retail, from the shop or by mail.

"There's no middleman involved in our operation whatsoever," Arval explained. "If we didn't run our own sawmill, we couldn't possibly sell at the prices we do."

The brothers know that sometimes a purchaser resells their chairs at double the price. Why not raise their own prices?

"We feel like that would be taking unfair advantage," said Arval. "We prefer to sell directly

With a heavy wooden mallet and a chisel made from an old auto spring, Edd Presnell roughs out a bowl—like the black-cherry dough bowl shown here—in his backyard at Banner Elk, North Carolina. He sold his first bowl in 1935 for a dollar; the one above brought him $75. Today he also makes dulcimers, goblets, biscuit cutters, and trays, invariably using native woods.

133

to our customers, as reasonably as possible, and not try to mass produce for a wholesale market."

Arval has no children; Walter's two daughters don't plan on keeping the shop; probably the brothers' apprentice will take over the business someday.

When I started investigating the continuity of crafts in the highlands, I thought I was looking for families who had been doing virtually the same type of work for many generations. Gradually I concluded that this was not a significant criterion. Families, and individuals, have been free to change; and naturally some have chosen to.

I had also decided that I ought to find evidence of a craft tradition wherever I went in the Ozarks or Appalachia. That theory held up, notably in the discovery of Dee Blair—experts had told me that Letcher County was not a noted crafts area.

I believe that anywhere in these highlands I can find people following crafts that are consistent with the tradition of crafts. Tradition of crafts—that's the proper way to express it. There are no purely traditional crafts outside museums.

If a craft is not contemporary in some respects, nobody will practice it. Methods and materials have altered; more frequently, motives have changed.

But does it matter that tourists buy the Ritchie sisters' cornshuck dolls? That Rex Harral makes spoons and tools to sell? That the best binder for Omah Kear's brooms is a commercial product? That Jakey Grider's woodcraft was not even thought of until a few years ago? Or that Buzz Cornelison's talents run to public relations?

Feeling for craft work runs deeper than this. I recognized it in the way Preston Blair caressed his old banjo, in Dee Blair's voice when he told me the bull tongue plow would not kill the soil. Nothing could express it better than the cheerful continuity of John Goodwin's daughter and grandchildren. The pricing policies of Walter Cornelison and the Woody brothers add a poignant commentary. Who will take up Helena Cross's work is open to conjecture. But it is open.

The tradition of crafts in the highlands continues. That which is outmoded elsewhere continues to be contemporary here. That which follows the old traditions most closely is often the most difficult to define beforehand.

One day when I was driving along a country road near Chestnutridge, Missouri, I noticed a beautiful new patchwork quilt a housewife was hanging on a clothesline. "It's sort of a friendship quilt," Helen Meier explained. "We made one just like it for Pastor Ledbetter about 20 years ago." Helen has been making quilts for about 50 years, for herself, her family, and for friends.

"Quilting is a lot of work," she remarked, "even working them up on the machine." I was alarmed for a tradition: patchwork quilts on a sewing machine!

But then, if pioneer women had had machines like Helen Meier's, would they have taken so many stitches by hand? Is that the most valuable part of the tradition, or is it laboriously turning scraps to good use? Or selflessly making gifts for loved ones?

I drove more than a hundred miles to see the turkey calls made by Herald and Kenneth Hughes, who live on a farm near Humansville, Missouri. Frankly, the workmanship disappointed me at first. But I made the mistake of looking when I should have been listening.

The brothers are ardent hunters; they make the calls strictly for sound to lure a gobbler. A beautifully finished turkey call that doesn't have a good sound is simply firewood to them.

Kenneth brought out a gun to show me and I was immediately impressed by the solid walnut stock. He had made it through long winter nights of patient labor. Ozarks men show off finely worked gunstocks to each other; they only listen to a turkey call.

On days when the acoustics of the North Carolina mountains are just right, you can stand in the gravel road that runs through the hollow where Willard and Ora Watson live and you can hear the hum of tourist traffic on the Blue Ridge Parkway. The distance is perhaps a mile . . . or a century. Willard and Ora have knowingly chosen to continue a way of life that they recognized early on as harsh.

Ora and her four sisters were motherless when she was two years old. Her father remarried, and had seven more children. Ora grew up working, taught herself to cook at a fireplace and to quilt.

Willard was raised by his grandparents, if age 14 is "raised." After that he went to work in the timber.

"I'm climbing 70 and never been in jail," says Willard. He wore brown kid slippers, white shirt, and "overhalls" when he and Ora were married "50 years ago last October."

Children? "There were six in our trap, and all knowed how to work." Willard himself used to work for eighty cents a day.

The Watsons "got by" tending a garden, milking a cow, raising and butchering hogs, selling witch-hazel leaves and sassafras bark, cutting wood and doing for themselves. They seldom wanted for food, nor did visitors to their home. That hasn't changed; and when Ora called the noon meal, Willard matter-of-factly insisted I join them. "We don't have much, but we never hide it from nobody."

I gorged myself on home-grown creamed potatoes, shellie beans and sliced onion, slaw with vinegar, biscuits and cornbread, honey and preserves.

Ora has made quilts all her life—for her own family, for her "young 'uns" when they left home, and for friends and neighbors. About ten years ago a visitor persuaded her to make some to sell, in patterns like Texas Star, Double Wedding Ring, and Monkey Wrench. She hasn't lacked a source of income since. (She did pull witch hazel worth $32 last summer, just to see what it was like to sell it at fifty cents a pound rather than a cent and a half, a price she remembers from years ago.)

The day I wandered down the gravel road, Willard had been up at four in the morning working in the weathered building with the sign that announces "Willard Watson's / Woodworks / Within."

Encouraged by folk-toy entrepreneur Jack Guy of Beech Creek, North Carolina, Willard began making wooden toys about ten years ago. He has picked up a pattern here and there, worked out many more on his own, varied them frequently. His toys would do credit to a trained engineer: a quartet of chickens alternately pecking feed from a bucket, a walking mule, a kicking pig, a climbing lizard, and dozens of others for young and old.

Willard won't belong to any organization or guild. "I can stay right at home here and do all I want to do. When I get behind real bad and everybody a-wantin' somethin', I get awful tired of it.

"It's just a matter of what you want to do. A satisfied mind is one of the finest things that's ever been. I work here. When I get tired, I don't have to ax my cap'n when I wanta go . . ."

It grew time for me to go. Ora was bending over the quilting frame. I set off along the winding gravel road, and Willard went up on the side of the mountain "to finish diggin' a row and a half of taters."

Stooped and bearded hillbilly character emerges from a block of wood in a sequence of carvings by Harold Enlow at Dogpatch, U.S.A.—an Arkansas amusement park. Sharon Copple of Branson, Missouri, did the portrait—only her second carving— of mountain man and friend Chic Allen.

Students, teachers, and artisans dance a "birdie in the cage" in the quadrangle of Fort New Salem, West Virginia, an authentic reconstruction of a frontier community. Craftsman Jerome Weaver carries a rocker and stools he made. A stomper doll, or limberjack, hangs waiting for a dance; its design dates from the early days of the country.

Stitching bright scraps into the Split Rail pattern, women of West Virginia work at a quilting frame of Civil War vintage: from left, Mrs. Fred Means (teacher), Mrs. Clayton Pinder, Lynn Barrington (students) at Salem College. Part-time teacher of a family tradition, Oral Nicholson completes a market basket of white oak. Student spinner, Mrs. Ivan Kovach twists local wool into thread at a wheel about 150 years old. The school's heritage arts program preserves these and similar skills once taken for granted in the region.

Working by sunlight on a half-completed churn, 84-year-old Alex Stewart of Sneedville, Tennessee, uses a croze to cut a groove that will hold the bottom in place. White-oak dasher and bands set off the red-cedar staves in the finished piece.

Master of the cooper's vanishing art, Alex Stewart straddles his shaving horse and fashions a churn stave with a drawknife. At right, above, he employs a round-shave to smooth the inside of a milk piggin, a vessel with one stave extended for a handle. "I make anything that can be made out of wood," he says, "and I don't use no nails nor glue." He owns power tools but prefers the tools he makes himself.

Handcrafted chair proves its sturdiness by supporting Arval Woody on one post. A fifth-generation chairmaker, Arval stages the demonstration for customers in the shop he and his brother, Walter, operate in Spruce Pine, North Carolina. Walter turns a chair leg on a lathe (top) and tapers the bottom with a gouge. Though all the posts appear identical, he produces them freehand, without measurement. Joints tighten over the years: The brothers insert kiln-dried ladders and rungs into less dry posts; as the posts dry further they shrink, clamping the rungs tighter.

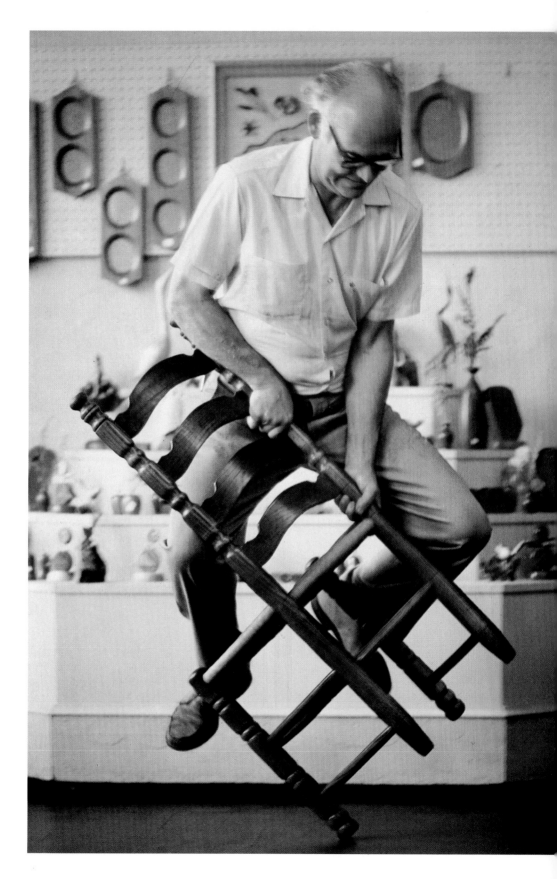

Like his great-grandfather before him, Walter Cornelison throws clay in Bybee,
Kentucky; here he adds spouts to half-gallon pitchers. Finished pieces gleam
near one of the kilns. A gradual deposit of dust and clay—like that coating
the telephone—has raised the floor of the shop several inches above its early-
19th-century level. A worker uses a jigger wheel (lower left) to make a pie plate.

Sharing their love of music, Stanley Hicks—who makes dulcimers—and Gretchen Corbitt—who is learning to play them—give an impromptu concert on Hicks's porch near Boone, North Carolina. A student at Appalachian State University, Gretchen visited Hicks for a special lesson. He spent a month in 1974 instructing students in the making and playing of dulcimers. At age 10, he helped his father make instruments, and has turned them out regularly himself for 20 years. Fretless banjos (below) also came from his shop. He makes them largely from black walnut and maple, and once used house-cat hides for the heads. "They'uz too many cats anyhow," he says. But then people "got fond of 'em," and he switched to groundhog skins.

*"You just can't keep a broom shop
clean," says Omah Kear. Here his
father, Elmer—patriarch of a
family broom-making enterprise near
Gatlinburg, Tennessee—works in a
litter of scraps. A grapevine handle
protrudes from the end, as Elmer
wraps broomcorn with fiber splits;
once he used poplar bark for the
binding. An estimated lifetime production of 200,000 brooms has
permanently warped his finger. He
began making brooms in 1928, and
sold them for 15 to 50 cents apiece.
Today Omah and a grandson help
in the shop, prices range from $3
to $10, and standards remain high:
"If you put out sorry stuff, you'll
ruin your trade," says Elmer.*

Toys: A Portfolio of Magic

UNCLE TOM WHITE whittled me toys from peach pits, the durable discarded seeds from the family orchard in King and Queen County, Virginia. The endless summer days of my

solitary childhood were filled with the buzzing of insects, the squeaks and squeals of Uncle Tom White's pocket-knife against the hard, crinkled pits.

He was my nurse as he had been my father's nurse before me. I always felt privileged to be with him, knowing that he was the oldest person alive and would people my play world with his tiny squirrels and monkeys, would delight me with his minute baskets that could really carry things.

Today I cannot look at a peach-pit monkey, an old scarred rocking horse, an incomplete Noah's Ark, or any handmade toy fragment of childhood without a feeling so poignant I am between tears and laughter.

Usually, and fortunately, homemade toys were simple. The imagination of the child supplied any finishing touches that the maker left out. Small replicas of grownup objects such as carts and wagons were plain enough to change form and function miraculously at the will of their little owners. With the simpler objects, children have more freedom to create — to make magic out of toy play.

Dolls were made of cornhusks, clay, wood, nuts, apples, stones swaddled in cloth, Indian beaded buckskin, and rags. One rag doll immortalized — and commercialized — in America during the 20th century was the intrepid Raggedy Ann.

Boys had toy soldiers and wooden guns, slingshots and Indian bows and arrows that really worked. Stuffed animals and beanbags and a hundred other delights kept boys and girls busy all during the week — until Sunday.

Often the Christian Sabbath would have

BY BEVERLY SPOTSWOOD

For Sunday play in the devout past: a barn-shaped Noah's Ark on wheels; its hinged roof lets the pairs of creatures go inside. For today: a peach-pit monkey whittled by Ozarkian Hobart Blair.

been longer, as children experience time, if it had not been for Noah's Ark, a "Sunday toy." Adult time and energy, and skill with a sharp knife, were the only limits to its array of animals. Because of its Biblical origin, Noah's Ark was a permissible plaything on this day of rest and duty — it taught sacred truths of religion.

For untold generations, in pueblos of the Southwest, Hopi and Zuni Indians have carved and painted the kachina dolls that represent spirits who take prayers to the gods. Fathers and uncles still give these dolls to young girls during annual ceremonies, and the dolls have special meaning — as did Noah's Ark, or the small wooden saints in the homes of Spanish descendants in New Mexico.

Giving children "the best we can afford" was a penchant of the first American colonists; it has persisted ever since, with unmistakable effects on our tradition of handcrafted playthings. If a settler could manage it, he bought a sophisticated toy from Europe. A loving Indian father might trade for European toys

as well as for other "civilized" goods; I have seen a 16th-century drawing of an Indian child holding an elaborate Elizabethan doll.

Toy making in America became a mechanized industry, but the handmade plaything never completely died. As late as the 1880's, vagabond carver Wilhelm Schimmel of Pennsylvania was whittling toys for farm children in the Cumberland Valley. In Appalachia and other regions where money for store-bought toys has always been scarce, a homemade toy tradition has flourished to this day.

Children play with flipperdingers and whimmydiddles, "buzz saws," Jacob's ladders, do-nothing machines, stomper dolls, pillars of Solomon, bull-roarers—imaginative names for simple mechanical toys made with a little skill, a little patience, and available materials like local wood, string, and maybe a bit of wire. If a weight is needed to make a chicken bob its head, a pebble will do.

Making even simpler toys can become a child's game in itself. Some good sturdy black-eyed peas, some clean broomstraw or tooth-picks, and a bit of paper are enough for furniture in miniature, assembled on the Tinkertoy principle. The pea—soaked beforehand, preferably overnight—serves as the element of joinery. Four peas are enough for a stool, with four straws for legs and four for the stretchers, a dab of raw egg for glue, and a square of paper for a seat. Even a paper doll might well be too heavy to sit on this, but it easily supports an elf!

Women all over the United States still make stuffed animals and rag dolls. A new surge of interest in doll houses challenges an increasing number of people to try building and furnishing in a one-inch-to-one-foot scale.

And toys of the past, more or less scuffed and worn, can be found in museums, private collections, or antique shops—often, of course, without clues to their former owners. It is difficult, however, to estimate the numbers of handmade playthings past or present, for more often than not one toy is made for one child. No one but me ever played with Uncle Tom White's peach-pit toys.

Overleaf: Miniature finery—fringed buckskin and beads, brass buttons and lace bonnet—clothes dolls of the 1880's or '90's. The Indian maid belonged to the family of a famed Shoshone chief, Washakie; a mother or aunt probably made it, adding a ten-inch lock of her own hair. Few rag dolls had such modish costumes as the one at left; often, especially on the frontier, mothers improvised playthings from the ragbag.

Dolls made of everyday items inspire a child's fantasies. Clockwise from upper left: A carved nut provides a head. Mrs. May Ritchie Deschamps of North Carolina produces dolls from cornshucks, with crocheted raffia trim. Dolls with dried-apple heads probably originated among the Iroquois; the maker pinches expressions into shape as the apples shrink. A new handmade Raggedy Ann—the heroine created by cartoonist Johnny Gruelle for his daughter in 1914—manages a wan smile after more than 50 years of loving. An elegant new rag doll sets forth in late Victorian garb; a carved wooden doll (below) has lost one cloth arm, part of her cotton wig.

Doll houses and furniture rival the real thing in craftsmanship and attention to detail. Alexandra Littlehales (opposite) helps builder David Althoz of Virginia fit the roof for a nearly completed model of her home; at a one-inch-to-one-foot scale, it even has glass windows that open and close. Below, a composite room includes several types of American furniture, accurately reproduced: Shaker chairs and stove share the simplicity of a punched-tin pie safe of 18th-century style. At right, a tiny pitcher and bowl, not from one set, reflect the care of the potter, possibly Pennsylvania German. In the days before illustrated catalogues, a salesman may have carried the Hitch-cock chair (upper right) as a sample. But most miniatures served as toys; and this one ended up, naturally and fittingly, in a children's toy collection.

As a favorite of toy maker and toy user, the horse has inspired playthings of varied style and function. The foot-tall pull toy below, made in New England or New York late in the 19th century, boasts leather ears and a genuine horsehair mane. About 1840, an unknown artist's "Boy in Plaid" played with a finely caparisoned hobby-horse probably imported from Europe. As the century passed, a flood of mass-produced toys from abroad affected local craftsmanship. The stylized wooden horse may represent an American's effort to compete by simplifying his work for quick production. But a mother, almost certainly, made the stuffed cloth horse as a cuddle toy. Bespotted and ragged, it proves the truth of one folklorist's comment: "...a toy in perfect condition is a pathetic thing. The toy which never knew the delight of a child has lost some of the essence that gives it meaning and genuine value."

BRETON LITTLEHALES

Toys of motion—push-pull type or weighted—
range from whittled twigs to intricate models.
Clothespin rider and rocking horse come from
North Carolina, as does the weighted "peck-a-
two"—if shaken, the chicks peck at the corn.
The wheeled rooster, Pennsylvania German,
dates from the 19th century. Students at Berea
College, Kentucky, made the Casey Jones
Special. Mountain laurel twigs form a "gee-haw
whimmydiddle": Rubbing the notched twig
with the smooth one turns the propeller
left or right. North Carolinian Willard Watson
made the precisely scaled walking mule and
wagon, more a showpiece than a toy.

Yesterday's techniques create dolls for today. A trained and practicing wood-carver and sculptor for 25 years, Marie Ferrian of Maryland turned to doll making only recently. She makes both wooden and ceramic models, but prefers working in wood. With her mallet and chisels she shapes a torso in "clear," or knotless, pine; later she adds wooden arms and legs, some hinged, some not. She fires her ceramic dolls in a kiln (below) before adding head, arms, and legs to a cloth body; then she paints the features with watercolors. Clothes, improvised from Marie's own garments, enhance a distinctive personality for "Charlie," a doll for the '70's (left). She wears a peasant blouse, blue jeans, a watchband belt, beads from Peru—and no shoes.

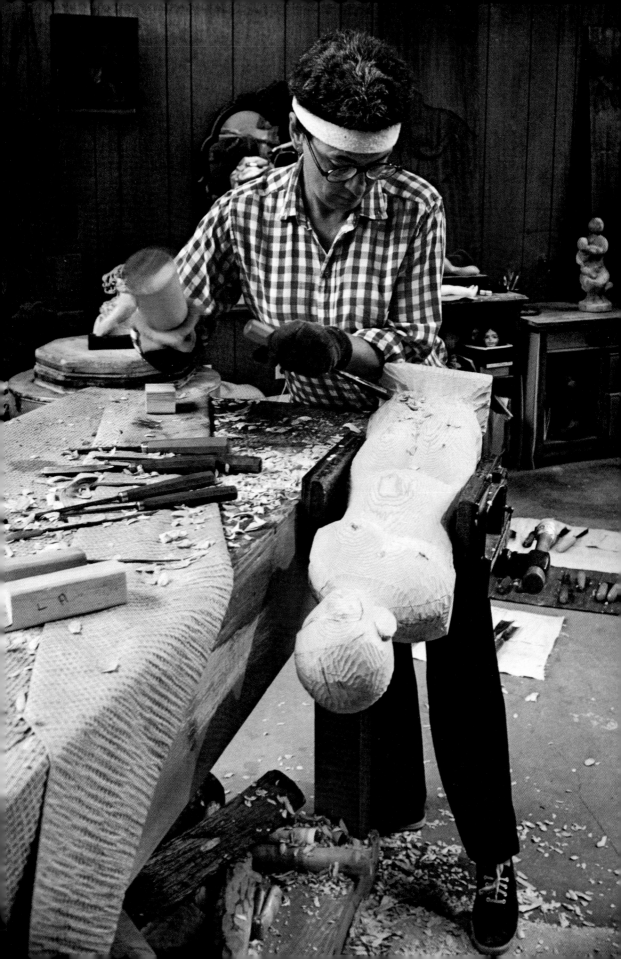

6

The Scene Today

I'D HARDLY EXPECTED TO FIND one of America's most inspirational craftsmen living in the midst of Manhattan, working in a converted shoe factory. But there she was, Lenore Tawney—a delicate and graceful woman in her 50's—creating fiber sculptures that hung like clouds from 20-foot ceilings.

Lenore, as I knew long before I met her, is an outstandingly innovative craftsman. She is of the generation that became involved in the art aspect of crafts years ago, before it had a following, a captive audience, a mass movement. As a weaver, she was creating gigantic three-dimensional fiber sculptures while others were still at the place-mat stage. At first some might have laughed or fumed, then they took notice, now they embrace her.

This is not simply because her works—some of them ethereal and serene; others earthy in form, bulky in weave—are so special. For nearly twenty years Lenore Tawney has embodied her personality in her work. Each thread, each knot, each feather becomes a part of the woman that is Lenore Tawney. And the woman, as she says herself, becomes each element in turn.

Like many of the craftsmen of the 1970's, she is as much a philosopher as an artist.

"I become timeless when I work with fiber. Each line, each knot is a prayer of sorts," she told me as we sipped her personal blend of herb tea from tiny cups created by a friend of hers, a potter.

"When you work, you must involve yourself totally. You can't be bored with your work. Because if you are bored, you put that boredom into the fiber, it stays there, becomes a part of that work. And that work then becomes everything you were at the moment you created it. If you were aware, involved during its creation, the work will be aware and involved. If you were bored, it will be forever boring."

Her philosophy, I thought, could apply to an auto mechanic, a business executive, an artist. She went on.

"I'm not a teacher, I've never taught formally except for one month at a spiritual center in New Mexico. For my work is very simple, nothing about it is really so complicated. Anybody can look at it and 'see' the techniques, use the same linen, the same colors."

She stopped for a moment and her brilliant blue eyes confronted me squarely.

"It's what you do with those materials that's important. You have to be in touch with yourself. When people ask me about my work, how I created it, I tell them, 'Don't look at other people's work for your creation, don't look outside, look in. If you look at other people's work, and not within yourself, you are only imitating. The challenge is, with each new work, to create a new part of yourself, a new being.'"

For three months I traveled from Deer Isle, Maine, to Julian, California, in search of the spirit of the American craftsman today. I could easily have traveled three times as long, from Hawaii to Florida or from Alaska to Georgia, without exhausting the crafts scene of the '70's. It includes county fairs and avant-garde galleries and church bazaars, street vendors' stands and world-famed museums. In the widest sense, it includes everyone who appears in this book.

Within one group alone I found an incredibly rich swatch of this nation's fabric—men and women who embody principles we romantic Americans like to see in our heritage.

They are hardworking, industrious. They convey a near-fanatical desire to create, to work with their hands. They prefer self-discipline to discipline from others, and live as intensely as they work.

I think they have reached what we all search for: a place in society where there is freedom; room for self-expression; self-satisfaction in their work; and, from time to time, a bit of public recognition.

I found their working days and nights long, at times tedious, at times euphoric. Sixteen-

BY PATRICIA L. RAYMER

Reflected in an ebony and ivory mirror of his creation, Frank Cummings typifies four aspects of today's craftsman: He teaches, at California State University, Long Beach; he experiments with a variety of materials, from amber to plastics; he draws upon themes and motifs of many cultures; and he furnishes his own home with his work.

hour stretches bent over a potter's wheel. Hours shaping molten globs of glass gathered from furnaces roaring at 2,000° F. Seemingly endless and inevitably boring hours tying knot after knot of fiber into wall hangings 30 feet long.

Some call themselves professional craftsmen, for this is how they make a living. Others prefer the term artist-craftsmen, emphasizing their interest in originality and form. On the whole, they are people who try to live by creating objects for others to enjoy.

They range in age from the 20's to the 80's. Some of their work is purely functional—frying pans, wooden tables. Some is purely esthetic—fabric wall hangings, glass sculptures. Yet each has blurred the fine line that once separated "craft" from "art," finding inspiration on either side.

Contemporary American pottery ranges from ovenproof kitchenware to austere cylindrical vases to satirical sculptures of sinks and toilets. Metalwork includes chalices for use in worship, functional sterling silver coffee sets, miniature toys filled with whimsy, elaborate bronze "body coverings." Fiberworks vary from simple place mats to "paintings" stitched with common cotton thread, from tapestries of traditional weave to hand-hooked carpets that resemble abstract paintings to wildly embroidered blue jeans.

As ceramist Erik Gronborg comments: "A generation raised on cars and television is no longer romantically inclined toward the natural primitive ways of the village potter in Japan and Mexico."

His colleagues prove his point; they're not afraid to be funny, or to make social comments. Rodger Lang pays good-humored tribute to the Beatles with four stoneware cups.

Goldsmith Bruce Clark of Tucson satirizes —in his words—"the white man's ripping off of Indian motifs," by mixing turquoise and silver with mild steel, coral, and copper for a "kitchen object" entitled Tacky Arizona Tourist Item. And J. Fred Woell of Deer Isle, Maine, produces an "antijewelry" pendant of plastic, walnut, and metal in honor of The Good Guys: Dick Tracy and Superman and Little Orphan Annie.

All told, craftsmen of the '70's refuse to limit their sources. They travel throughout the world to learn from their fellow craftsmen, returning home to revive old techniques or expand traditional dimensions. They take much of their imagery from cultures past or distant: heavily laden neckpieces that echo the Bronze Age, fabrics that develop Persian themes, pots that translate the eloquent simplicity of pre-Columbian or African art.

These craftsmen have no fear of combining Space Age materials and Stone Age techniques, or vice versa. A potter may throw a classical vase, then embellish it with a "pop" photographic image. A weaver may take an ancient loom technique and weave a translucent sculpture of common fishing line.

In short, many feel confined by traditional standards and attempt to break away, and come up with a style at once classic and contemporary and distinctively American.

More often than not, the professional craftsman came to his career quite by accident. Many began as engineers, industrial designers, English teachers. But they were drawn to the crafts out of a shared desire for independence, a need "to be my own boss," a passion to experiment; and these common threads bind them emotionally.

After meeting many, I think it's safe to say that they make up a national subculture. Their uniform is a blue work shirt and faded Levi's. They get together at summer craft fairs to meet old friends, catch up on one another's work, share in failures and successes. Some

have their own organizations, such as GAS, the Glass Art Society, and SNAG, the Society of North American Goldsmiths.

Few make a lot of money, even in boom times. Many rely on teaching for a steady basic income. And what they don't sell in the marketplace, they barter—a ceramic cup for a small woven pillow, a silver necklace for a carefully crafted dining-room chair.

"I'm constantly trading my work," one California potter told me. "I've never paid a dental bill in my life; they always accept a plate or a cup in exchange. Unfortunately, I've never found a car dealer who'd do the same!"

Some live in homes filled with their own creations and those of their friends. Others live in near austerity, giving away or selling each object as soon as it's finished.

"I like to live simply," metalsmith Fred Fenster told me one day. An art professor at the University of Wisconsin-Madison, Fred lives in a renovated cheese factory outside the town. His house is sparsely furnished: a bed, some cooking utensils, metalworking tools.

"All I need to live are my tools and myself. Whatever I don't make for commission— mostly wedding bands—I give away."

He brought out an elegant, hammered copper cooking pot he had just completed and was about to give to a close friend.

"Somebody asked me what this pot would cost. I couldn't sell it for less than $500, just considering the time and materials. Nobody would spend $500 on a copper cooking pot, and I'm not the kind of guy that could sell it for that. But I guess I am the kind of guy that could give it away."

Then, a bit nostalgically, and with an obvious sense of pride, he lifted the lid and, in mime, sniffed the pot.

"But I have to admit, it sure is great to cook a bit of chicken in wine in this, and know you're eating out of a $500 pot!"

As that "price" indicates, the craftsman's role in American society has changed: from that of the only person who supplied necessary utilitarian objects for the marketplace to one who offers creations even the most advanced technology could not provide—a skillfully, lovingly wrought one-of-a-kind item without the anonymity of the mass-produced object, without built-in obsolescence.

And, as the American love affair with the mechanized world began to wane, handmade became synonymous with well-made.

Between the great Centennial celebration

of 1876 and World War I, Americans turned with sympathy to the arts and crafts movement that had begun in England. This foreshadowed the current crafts revolution. But why, I wondered, did the crafts scene change so dramatically in the past few decades?

During the 1920's there were few artist-craftsmen as we know them today. By the 1930's, scattered throughout the country, metalsmiths, weavers, and potters were developing the new definition of crafts even while the Great Depression gave traditional crafts a new importance for many. Handmade eel spears or mittens from New England, handmade brooms from the southern highlands—anything that might earn a little money gained importance when millions were out of work. Federal agencies did their best to help local craft enterprises, setting a precedent for projects that sustain craftwork today.

Escaping Nazi persecution and other perils of war, distinguished craftsmen from Europe sought refuge in America in the '30's and '40's, bringing assured skill and new perspectives of art. The revolution gained new recruits during the 1940's, with servicemen coming home from World War II.

"There was an incredible spirit after the war," metalsmith Ronald Hayes Pearson told me. "We knew we just didn't want to go back to factories and offices, nine to five. We'd all had a lot of time to think about what we wanted to do; we'd already lost a big chunk of time out of our lives. Since then I've never seen quite the same determination to get something out of school."

Hundreds, like Ron Pearson, returned to the universities on the GI bill, demanding courses in art and in the crafts. Schools that had no classes in pottery, weaving, metal, soon began seeking out the few available craftsmen to teach. Before long, the ceramics studio was as much a part of many campuses as the biology lab.

Pearson, now entering his 50's, is typical of this "first generation" of contemporary craftsmen. When he left school trained as a metalsmith, he faced a world ill-equipped to deal with a man who wanted to make a living as one pair of hands.

In 1948, when he set up his first metal shop in an abandoned chickenhouse in Alfred, New York, he had no galleries ready to display his craftwork and no stores to sell it, no contemporary standards and little tradition for handmade metal objects. And few craftsmen with

Revolutionary talents vitalize two crafts. At San Ildefonso Pueblo about 1919, Maria Martinez (above) and her late husband, Julian, revived a type of prehistoric pottery now world-famous. Near-perfect finish, and the black-on-black contrast of matte surface on brilliant polish, distinguished theirs from all other blackware. In 1957 Lenore Tawney moved into a New York City loft and began weaving. As her skill grew, her innovations—and her influence—multiplied. "Each line, each knot is a prayer of sorts," says this philosopher-artist.

KATHY ANDRISEVIC (ABOVE AND LEFT)

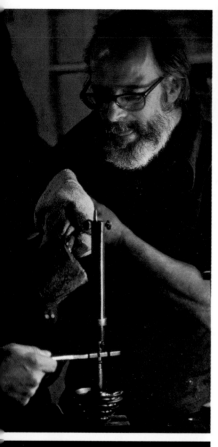

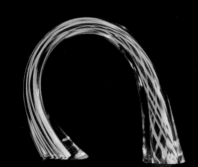

NATIONAL GEOGRAPHIC PHOTOGRAPHER BATES LITTLEHALES (ABOVE)

"Glass wants to do what liquids do — to flow freely and smoothly," says Dominick Labino, whose *"Emergence XV"* (right) spreads growing ripples of translucence. Labino, an authority on glass chemistry, has turned to free-blown glass as an art form, inspiring others. One — Tom McGlauchlin, who made the vase at left — starts a bubble of molten glass on his blowpipe at the Fenton Art Glass factory in Williamstown, West Virginia. Another, Jack Ink, engraves a design with a copper wheel. A noted teacher, Harvey Littleton (far left), works with a teacher of his own, Max Erlacher from Steuben Glass, in his studio at Verona, Wisconsin; there he made the sculpture *"Loop,"* characteristic of his recent work.

whom to share the creative dialogue that all artists need.

For years he made hand-raised silver hollow ware that no one would buy, earned an income with spun bronze hollow ware that did sell, and created some jewelry.

"When I look back at the work I did then, I realize it was awful," Pearson acknowledges with a laugh. "We didn't know what we were doing. We had no background, no tradition. Today, it takes a student two or three years to learn technically what it took us a decade or more to put together."

During the days Pearson spent in his chickenhouse, few practicing craftsmen even tried to live by their work, and those who did found it hard.

"About the most valuable thing a craftsman of the 1950's could have was a list of the few shops around the country that would buy his work outright," Pearson explains. Maybe because of his struggle, or maybe in spite of it, he is now one of the country's most revered and most successful metalsmiths.

Secluded on a scantily populated island off the Maine coast, he operates one of the few American metal shops run on an apprentice-master basis. With seven paid apprentices—some are trained by Pearson, some come with art-school background—he turns out about 200 handmade creations a week: mainly rings, earrings, bracelets, and neckbands. The eight market the jewelry to about 30 shops throughout the nation, and have a tough time keeping them supplied.

Although it took him more than twenty years, Pearson has found what he set out for: "I always said I could live anywhere where I could get to a post office now and then and ship off my work. I guess I've proved you can do it!"

While the craftsmen of Pearson's era did not simply create a demand for craft objects, they have created a climate of acceptance, understanding, and appreciation. Over the years they have set the scene, establishing standards, developing a tradition, and organizing a network of communication that was nonexistent in the 1950's.

So, when metalsmith Ellen Reiben Posilkin graduated from the University of Wisconsin in 1972, at the age of 21, she pretty much took it for granted that she would be able to make some sort of living at her craft. She had learned about marketing techniques, and discussed with fellow students and professors the ways "to make a go of it"—apprenticeships, designing a line of jewelry for production, joining a crafts cooperative.

"I knew I still had a lot to learn, but I knew that if I really wanted it and worked hard enough, there was no question that I'd make it—and, hopefully, that I'd never have to take a side job as a secretary or something."

Today Ellen works out of The Craftsmen of Chelsea Court, a shop in Washington, D. C. It sells works by more than a hundred professional craftsmen from all over the country, and supplies studio space for nearly two dozen who live in the area.

She pays no rent for her studio, but gives a percentage of her profits on sales to the store. Like her fellow craftsmen there—who work in metal, fiber, stained glass, leather, and clay—Ellen is completely on her own in accepting commissions or creating and executing her work, but gains exposure to the public and companionship among her peers.

"We've all been talking about the economic situation recently," says Ellen; "I have weaving friends who are really having a hard time. Weaving takes so long—jewelry's quicker. But I can't think of a better life for me; I price my own work, and if I feel like making rings one day and a bracelet the next, I'm free to do it. All I need now is for a rich patron to walk into the store, and I'm all set!"

Luxury crafts, notably glassblowing, have always demanded rich patrons; and for generations America did not have enough of them to sustain the craftsman who produced one-of-a-kind objects in glass. The United States' early contribution to glass lay in simplified production for lower prices. American firms eagerly adopted the long-familiar three-part molds that speed up the glassblower's work, and the new pressing machines, developed in the 1820's, that eliminated it.

In recent years, industry, universities, and museums have acted as generous patrons for artist-craftsmen in glass, as Harvey Littleton's career reveals. He grew up in Corning, New York, where his father was director of research for Corning Glass Works, and served in World War II—craftsmen of that generation, he says, came home to work "with the same determination we had used in France and the South Pacific."

He took leave in 1957 from the University of Wisconsin, where he had been teaching ceramics. With a small travel grant from the university research committee, he set off to study Moorish influence on the pottery of Spanish villages.

"I went to Europe," he recalls, "and when I visited Paris I found one glassblower who had been working alone in his studio, creating beautiful works. He gave me a couple of his old tools, and eight months later I returned home to experiment." At first his new glass lab was his own garage.

Toledo, Ohio, proudly calls itself the industrial glass capital of the world; the Toledo Museum of Art has a superb collection of glass; and in 1962 Littleton proposed a Toledo seminar on molten glass as a medium for the artist-craftsman.

The museum acted as sponsor. Dominick Labino, then vice president and director for research at Johns-Manville Fiber Glass, Inc., modified a furnace and supplied some glass for experiments. And Harvey Leafgreen, a retired glassblower from the Libbey Glass Company, brought the technical expertise of a veteran to the enterprise.

"Leafgreen's one of the old-timers," says Tom McGlauchlin, who attended that first seminar and now runs the museum's new glass studio. "He started learning glassworking as a boy in Sweden—he's 81 now. He dropped in at the first meeting, wearing a dark suit and tie, and ended up showing us how to apply some of the tricks of the trade. He still comes in when he feels like it, to make Christmas presents or give the students some tips."

From that beginning, which produced some lopsided, thick, and bubble-marked pieces, came rapid development, with experimental workshops springing up around the country. In 1962 the University of Wisconsin set up the first university course in glassblowing. Today more than 50 American schools, from Providence, Rhode Island, to the Cascade wilderness north of Seattle, offer glass as another medium for young artists to explore.

Retired since 1965, Dominick Labino has built a studio on his farm near Grand Rapids, Ohio, designing his own furnaces and annealing ovens for a full-time career with hot glass as an art medium. "A glass worker of 2,000 years ago could walk into my shop and feel quite at home," he has said. "Basic tools and methods have changed very little." But he brings a thoroughly contemporary mastery of glass chemistry to his quest for lovely forms and subtle coloring.

Still teaching at the University of Wisconsin,

Harvey Littleton lives on a hundred-acre farm outside Madison; and he stresses a lack of tradition in glass as an American artist's asset, a source of freedom for a pioneer. "My work is not rooted in the 18th century," he told me. "The greatest thing about American craft is that it is not rooted in craft, but in art."

In the shop talk of technical problems, artist and artisan of any craft can find common ground—a point made clear at Williamstown, West Virginia, over the Memorial Day weekend of 1974.

Normally the Fenton Art Glass Company there turns out items for the novelty and souvenir trade, and such accessories as "Burmese decorated lamps" for gift shops. With the cooperation of the American Flint Glass Workers Union, the owner held open house on the holiday for the annual meeting of GAS as well as for employees and their guests.

Costume distinguished the two groups beyond possible confusion. The glass artists, men and women, appeared in well-worn blue jeans; most of them had kerchiefs or headbands to keep long hair back from annealing ovens at a mere 900° F. or pots of glass molten at something more than 2,000°.

Close-cropped and close-shaven, the employees preferred crisp chino trousers and sports shirts. The younger women with them wore slacks or pastel miniskirts with white high-heeled shoes. Older women wore sensible dresses—and kept ever-watchful eyes on children who might stray too close to a furnace or a "gather" of molten glass in transit on the end of a blowpipe from furnace to workbench.

At first the two groups seemed to keep apart by unspoken agreement. The company men entertained family and friends, molding glass leaves or blowing small pitchers. One, built like a tackle from a pro football team, produced some tiny red glass frogs; another, lean and rangy, delighted a circle of children with miniature pulled-glass horses.

The artists tried any sort of item, from straightforward stemmed dish to improvised whatchamacallit. A New York lawyer devoted himself to a glass biplane worthy of Snoopy or the Red Baron. All of them admired the up-to-date Fenton facility; one declared happily, "It's like playing Yankee Stadium after Little League!"

As the afternoon wore on, with craftsmen cheerfully fooling around with hot glass, members of the two groups began comparing methods, discussing techniques, and collaborating on glasswork of finely mixed idiom.

Some of the GAS people shaped a freeform white container; one shouted, "Where are the owls? Hurry with the owls. . . ." The burly Fentonian charged up with three fire-hot red glass owls on a metal plate. The owls were promptly perched under the container to serve as "feet." And all involved congratulated themselves at a high point in a day full of fun.

While the professional craftsman embraces glass, metal, or wood as part of his life and life-style, thousands of Americans find similar self-fulfillment on a part-time scale. Call them "weekend" or "Sunday" craftsmen, but they share the artist's sense of worth and joy in creating something from start to finish with their own hands.

This proliferation of crafts in America responds to many factors in 20th-century experience. It's part of the "back to the earth" movement and a desire to return, if only for a few hours, to a simpler life. It's part of the increase in leisure that a complex modern society has provided.

It's an escape from a sense of personal obsolescence, for some. "After all," one man told me with a laugh, "when you retire from the car business, you can't sit around for the next twenty years thinking about how to make a better fender."

For many, it's a reaction against machine-made objects that lack esthetic appeal and lack sturdiness and often cost too much.

And for many it's also an attempt to get a little closer to a heritage that seems to have gotten lost in the shuffle.

As the first Centennial inspired fresh attention to crafts, Americans approaching a second grand anniversary turn to crafts for a fresh understanding of origins, a new gauge of accomplishment.

Affirmation of a heritage inspires some. Women whose grandmothers may have never even picked up a needle are creating quilts of their own. Japanese-Americans create delicate hand-fired pots that echo an oriental culture, and black Americans take to tie-dyeing techniques perfected in West Africa.

Crossing cultural borders inspires others. White Americans, who may have never even met an Indian, build Navajo looms and learn weaving techniques "from the book."

Moreover, the current emphasis on liberation for both sexes allows men and women to explore craft fields "closed" to them in the past. Businessmen zoom along in jet planes not the least embarrassed by the needlepoint in their laps—possibly a design by Rosey Grier, formerly a professional football star. Women fill woodworking courses or take up the hammer in a blacksmith shop without worrying about being "unfeminine."

Across the land today, in conventional classrooms, in converted garages, in craft schools like Haystack at Deer Isle, Maine, or Penland in the North Carolina mountains, thousands of Americans attend classes in weaving, pottery, metalsmithing, glassblowing. Informal lessons—with friends or neighbors—defy any attempt at counting.

In many cases, would-be craftsmen are turned away at the door—there just aren't enough offerings to meet the growing demand. For example, in 1973 there were more than 600 applications for the 300 slots at the 25-year-old Haystack Mountain School of Crafts on Deer Isle. But the 300 who were able to share the "Haystack experience" came to do more than learn to weave or throw a pot.

"At Haystack, we're as interested in spiritual experience as in producing craftsmen—in showing what working with the hand can do for the soul," says the school's director, Francis Merritt.

Each summer, this arcadian 63-acre school overlooking the waters of East Penobscot Bay bustles with a free-school spirit that brings together a highly varied group. Psychiatrists take a few weeks off to take up pottery. Housewives leave children at home with Dad to build their own looms. Elementary-school teachers come, hoping to take back something new to the classroom next fall. A museum curator, who spends the year handling rare and precious pottery, comes to learn for herself what the art demands. And professionals come to learn new techniques in their own crafts or to dabble in a new one.

Over the years, most of them have been from the 50 states; about 5 percent, from Canada. Some are from Europe; others from Tanzania or Nigeria, from Israel, Brazil, Japan, Australia.

Those who can manage it keep coming back. One retired Canadian couple returned to Haystack for 13 years running. They quit only when they reached their 80's.

Across the continent in Berkeley, California, a different sort of craft school grew out of a community need. Since 1973, a group of University of California graduates have operated Fiberworks, offering short-term workshops, full-fledged courses for academic credit, and special lectures.

"We really run a nonprofit salon of sorts," explains the founder, 31-year-old Gyöngy (Ginger) Laky. "Textile work is a solitary art— we set this place up not only as a school, but also to give people a place to come together to work, to experiment with new looms, new methods, new materials."

She stresses this point: "Knowledge in textiles doesn't change much; techniques may go unchanged for centuries. But we like to bring history into the thing, not work in a cultural vacuum. A kimono's more than so much silk —it's a whole cultural expression."

In its brief existence, Fiberworks has grown from a school with a few courses in elementary weaving to one with several dozen courses in almost every known aspect of fiber and fabric. Its pupils study kimonos, old-fashioned American quilting, Egyptian mordant textile printing, Latin American backstrap-loom construction, Southeast Asian *ikat* dyeing.

At Mineral Point, Wisconsin, an old Cornish mining town snuggled in some of the nation's most productive farmland, Ken Colwell is fulfilling a lifelong dream.

"Ever since I was a kid, I wanted a loom. I like machinery, I like to build things, and— well, looms were handsome and they were machines and they gave you the power to create beautiful objects," Colwell told me. So, when he got to college, he managed to sandwich a home economics weaving course or two into his load of psychology studies. That was nearly 30 years ago.

As a pastime, over the years, he bought up old looms, repaired them, experimented with the various fabrics they could make. Soon he was collecting pre-Civil War coverlets, tapestries, flags—all the fabrics weavers had fashioned on these same looms.

In 1968 he bought the town's abandoned Mineral Springs Brewery, renovated it, and set up a museum for his collection. Now he operates regular weaving workshops, with old looms and new. Students come from throughout the Midwest and as far as California to share his "hobby."

Lighting a burly old pipe, the 52-year-old administrator looked at me reflectively, and smiled. "I guess I've made a pretty deliberate decision that this would be a second career. I've been a bureaucrat long enough. I believe

Keeping alive a tradition of fine handmade Western saddles, ex-rancher Milton D. Rust of Colorado stitches a nearly completed model—one of hundreds he has made. Marylander Rudolf P. Bahr re-creates Kentucky rifles and antique pistols; he buys the rifled barrels, does some of the metalwork and all of the woodwork himself.

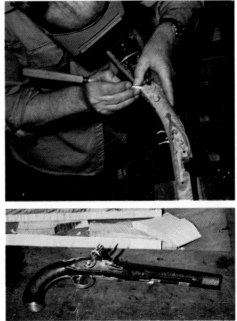

173

I ought to do, at least at this stage of my life, what I really want to do—create beautiful objects with my hands, and teach others."

Every Thursday night in Bloomfield Hills, Michigan, a varied group of men leave their daily jobs behind and sit themselves down at workbenches in Professor Richard Thomas's metal studio at Cranbrook Academy of Art. They include an auctioneer, a surgeon, a metal dealer; they make a silver pitcher, a gold ring for a friend, a chalice, a bronze vase.

Sixty-year-old James Howarth has worked with metal all his life. As a self-employed dealer in used machinery, he had a good idea what metal was all about. Or so he thought.

He stopped work to talk with me, a wooden-handled raising hammer in one hand, a half-completed silver wine cup in the other. "I never believed you could make such beautiful things with such simple tools. And the metal, it's so elastic, it bends at your command!"

Howarth has belonged to the class since it began in 1970. Since then, he has spent nearly ten hours a week discovering a new world of metal at his bench.

"It makes me so proud," he said excitedly. "My friends—they admire my work greatly—and what satisfaction in knowing I made it myself, with my own hands, and a little help from these tools.

"Quite frankly, before I got into this thing, I never cared to go to museums. Just didn't have much interest. But now, wherever I go, whenever I travel, I visit museums and respect and admire what I see. Because I know what's transpired, I know the hours and the love it took to create these beautiful objects."

Dr. James Wells is a professor of botany at Cranbrook. For the past three years, metal has been his "outlet."

"Let's face it, having a chance to work with your hands—it's very rewarding—and it sure cuts down on the psychiatry bills.

"I saw this as a rare opportunity—it's like living in the past." His gesture led my eyes to the studio's array of equipment: leather sandbags, mallets, assorted hammers, mandrels, T-stakes, vises, machine tools. "I guess I like living in the past. I'm not ready to capitulate to this world of hamburgers, french fries, and stainless steel."

Wells fondled his handmade silver water pitcher: "You know, you couldn't go uptown and buy this for any price. There's only one like it in the world!"

When 64-year-old Leo Winston, a retired automotive engineer, joined the class, he thought it might be a good hobby.

"After I'd been in class six months, I decided this was for me." And in the spring of 1974 Cranbrook awarded him the master of fine arts degree in metalsmithing.

Now he works at his newfound career. He has exhibited jewelry and silver and bronze hollow ware at local galleries. "Grant a man and his wife all the options retirement brings," he said, "add to that a new career—and you'll never be bored a day in your life."

In pioneer times and prehistory, boom years and bust, good craftsmanship has served the peoples of America; but the crafts scene today is one of unique richness, drawing strength from more traditions than the most gifted workers of the past could know. And, as James Howarth says, to learn something of one aspect of crafts is to find new pleasures waiting in the others.

James Hubbell's life bears this out; I can only describe him as a "supercraftsman," at once professional and amateur. His versatility is reminiscent of Revere's. He is architect, interior designer, bricklayer, stained-glass window-maker, metalsmith, furniture designer, roofer, sculptor, engineer, tile-setter . . . and the list goes on.

Since 1958, Hubbell has combined all his skills and talents in designing and constructing a fantastic fairyland sort of "village" for his wife, Anne, and four sons, ages 6 to 16. Situated on a dozen rugged acres of southern California countryside, his home is actually five hand-crafted buildings and a mosaic-tiled swimming pool. Each building blends easily and naturally with the hillsides, the dusty-green live oaks, the Western skies.

"It is not really a question of why I built this house the way I did. For I had no choice, it grew out of its environment," the 42-year-old craftsman told me in soft and modest tones.

As we wandered through his compact "village," I hardly knew where to look first. The details astonished me. Hand-forged handles on hand-carved doors. Store-bought bathroom handbasins, fully functional, reincarnated with meticulous tile settings. Hand-wrought copper gargoyles on the eaves. Simple and sturdy hand-built beds, and sofas. Hubbell sculptures atop a grand piano, in a fireplace niche. Brilliantly colored stained-glass windows everywhere, catching the noonday California sun "just right."

Hubbell built the "rooms" of his house one

by one, as a 17th-century New Englander might have enlarged his father's clapboard dwelling or a 19th-century settler might have added to his first hastily reared log cabin. The adobe building that once served the whole family is now a study. There's one structure for sleeping, one for eating and relaxing, one for a workshop, one for storage. Currently Hubbell is putting up another for his older sons: bedrooms, a bath, a kitchenette.

"I started out just wanting to build a house; I never imagined it would come to this," he laughed. "It's really a disease, building—the new addition is just an excuse."

Tall of frame, short-haired and blue-eyed, Hubbell was trained as a painter and a sculptor but could not confine his energy to any single art. "I've got an overactive thyroid," he concluded jokingly.

He shares with his fellow craftsmen past and present a sense of industry, of making do, an ability to create something out of virtually nothing. Much of the material in his buildings came from scrap piles: discarded bricks, broken pieces of colored glass, lumber no one knew what to do with.

Such a blend of inspiration and thrift produced some of the most appealing craftwork in the American tradition. In a similar fashion a villager in New Mexico might make a shrine for the family's patron *santo* with metal from tin cans the "Yankee" newcomers threw away.

Jim Hubbell doesn't confine his talents to the home; he doesn't want to and couldn't afford to. "I figure I spend about one-third of the time building, one-third of the time making sculptures and painting, and one-third of the time making a living," he explained. He earns his income as a designer, a tile-layer, a maker of stained glass. His creations fill churches, office buildings, restaurants, and homes around the San Diego area.

In addition to everything else, I found in Hubbell a poet and a philosopher, with goals worthy of a country's study.

"I wish that man could live in homes as marvelous and beautiful as that of a snail, that he could build cities as endlessly rewarding as a forest."

But most of all, Hubbell is a craftsman and an artist imbued with a strong love for the world around him.

"You need not understand beauty to create it," he said softly. "But to find it, you must worship it. For me, the joy of creating is synonymous with the joy of living."

Weaving a link with her ancestors, Mary Jane Bennett works at a roadside stand in South Carolina. She produces baskets derived from those made in West and Central Africa generations ago, following similar forms and patterns and using the coiling technique. On an offshore island, Harold Rouse gathers sweet grass that the local basketmakers will stitch with torn strips of palmetto frond.

"You need not understand beauty to create it," says James Hubbell, who has made a career of doing both. Trained as a painter and sculptor, versatile as a craftsman, he has scattered his home over 12 rural acres of southern California. Five adobe structures—one for sleeping, one for eating and relaxing, a study, a workshop, a storeroom—stand near a swimming pool. A sixth will provide a kitchenette and bedrooms for two older sons. Here, by his shop, the builder works with mallet and chisel on an abstract form in black walnut. "I use redwood a lot, cedar, sometimes avocado—whatever I can get," he comments. He supports his family by making stained glass on commission, by sculpture, and by architecture. Below, son Drew, age 13, cleans the pool. At left, California sun lights a Hubbell-made window in the studio bathroom.

NATIONAL GEOGRAPHIC PHOTOGRAPHER BATES LITTLEHALES

JONATHAN BLAIR

*Self-taught furniture maker Wendell Castle carves a
dining room table from a chunk of laminated maple in
his shop at Scottsville, New York. Six to ten coats of
hand-rubbed oil will finish the piece. He uses the
chair at left, of laminated white oak, in his own home.
An incidental discovery determined his career — he found
he could sit on a sculpture, slightly modified, that he
made as a graduate student at the University of Kansas.*

NATIONAL GEOGRAPHIC PHOTOGRAPHER BATES LITTLEHALES

Lissome-lady jewelbox in Guatemala hardwood holds one drawer within another in her abdomen; a third emerges from her head. Arthur Carpenter, known professionally as Espenet, finishes the piece in his California studio. Self-taught in woodworking, he lists utility, durability, a finish pleasing to the touch and to the eye, and economy of materials as his objectives. He made the walnut "wishbone" chair in 1974.

Weaving merges into sculpture as craftsmen develop novel forms with techniques as familiar as knitting or plaiting. Fiber artist Ron Goodman of Washington, D. C., crochets before one of his environmental sculptures—he adjusts the hanging of such a piece to fit its setting. Kay Sekimachi (left) of California constructs airy hangings from nylon monofilament fishing line.

A pioneer in this field, Californian Barbara Shawcroft (above) makes large off-loom woven works in three full dimensions; clowning, she nearly disappears into one of them.

181

Erik Gronborg, here shaping a pot in his San Diego workshop, considers contemporary images highly significant in his work: "cars, stock market graphs, photos of girls." A 1959 immigrant from Denmark, he studied in California. He combines techniques in novel ways—on this teapot, he applied low-fired luster glazes over porcelain. "The finished work that satisfies the artist is what counts," he says. A craftsman, in his words, "takes the same care with his art as with repairing his son's bicycle."

Considering all art self-portraiture, Robert Arneson cheerfully features his own likeness in much of his work. Ear-like handles add whimsy to a face-jug; below, he sculpts a larger-than-life study of his head. He startled the craft world with the zany humor of funk, a far-out movement of the '60's: ceramic six-packs, toothbrushes, bathroom fixtures, typewriters with keyboards of red-nailed fingertips. Recently he spent two years on ceramic and watercolor renderings of his California home. He wants, he says, an America of craftsmen who appreciate the world's beauties—and its absurdities.

Like many contemporary ironworkers, Albert Paley (above) began as a goldsmith, then became interested in the "inherent plasticity" of iron. Here, in his smithy at Rochester, New York, he works on iron gates for the Smithsonian Institution's Renwick Gallery in Washington, D.C. Brent Kington of Makanda, Illinois, forged the abstract weather vane of mild steel and embossed the copper "sail." Bea Hensley, who learned ornamental ironwork from Daniel Boone VI, made the rooster in the forge he shares with his son in Spruce Pine. The hammered copper saucepan—with pewter lining and forged iron handle—comes from the Syracuse workshop of Michael Jerry; he uses it and a matching skillet in his kitchen.

Cascading fabric clothes a wall in the San Francisco studio of Marsha Nygaard. This hanging illustrates a recent development in crafts: the movement away from the functional—everyday utensils and implements—to the purely decorative. Here she works with old furs scavenged from flea markets and thrift shops. "Maybe recycling them preserves the animals' souls," she says. Long a favorite garb of students and street people, blue jeans have recently become canvases for amateur artists. In 1973, Levi Strauss & Co. sponsored a Denim Art Contest that drew 2,000 entries, including those below. Artists used everything—paint, studs, feathers, buttons, shells, chevrons, lace, ribbons, medals, bottlecaps, bicycle chains, and wig samples—to decorate their jeans and jackets. Many embroidered their designs; some used needlepoint, crochet, and appliqué. Fifty prize-winning garments have toured museums at home and abroad, attracting—and amusing—crowds everywhere.

N.G.S. PHOTOGRAPHER OTIS IMBODEN (BELOW)

THOMAS L. AND STEFANIE C. DAVIES (BELOW)

KATHY ANDRISEVIC (BELOW)

Tomorrow's craftsmen absorb skills from the past in classes around the nation. Master weaver Janet Taylor (crouching) explains fine points of warp and weft to a student at Penland School of Crafts in North Carolina. Pima Indian Madeline Lewis (top) teaches basketry at the Museum of New Mexico in Santa Fe. Apprentice boat-builder Robert Monroe works on a stem-rabbet, where planking fits into the keel, at Bath, Maine. Summer student Miki Conn finishes a coiled pot at the Haystack Mountain School of Crafts at Deer Isle, Maine; a teacher from Nigeria gave the course, featuring African heritage in American crafts.

Contemporary ornaments reveal the diversity of materials
and techniques used by today's craftsmen. Ronald Pearson's
forged gold necklace (upper left) separates into two sections
of nuggets. As one of the first artists to adopt an industrial
process, electroforming, Stanley Lechtzin avoided the weight
of solid metal in his hollow torque of silver-gilt and cast
polyester. Svetozar Radakovich used the ancient lost-wax
process on parts of his feathered gold necklace. Pheasant
and rooster feathers on Frank Cummings's gold necklace
contrast with ivory and pearl. Albert Paley designed a
27-inch pendant — of forged metals, carved ivory, stone,
and glass — hinged for flexibility. An unknown contemporary
Indian of New Mexico's Santo Domingo Pueblo employs
his tribe's classic inlay with turquoise, jet, and mother-of-
pearl on a shell from the West Coast. For an archaic effect,
Imogene Gieling fused small sheets of torn silver to form
hollow beads, washed them with gold, and completed
her necklace with bright disks of Italian coral.

Linking past and future, Charles Loloma develops a Hopi tradition to craft timeless jewelry—like the ring and bracelets below. In his studio high in the desert country of Arizona, he works with gold and silver, coral, turquoise, ironwood, ivory, and lapis lazuli.

N.G.S. PHOTOGRAPHER OTIS IMBODEN (ABOVE AND BELOW)

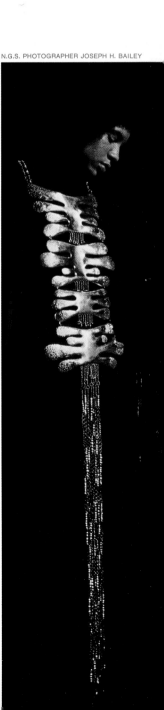

As the scene today becomes the scene tomorrow, Arline Fisch constructs jewelry that extends the frontiers of craftsmanship. A model stands draped in one of her creations—a body ornament of hammered silver. At right, Arline checks a pendant she has just finished; she wears each new piece as a final test of "rightness." Research into the ornaments of ancient and primitive cultures provides the inspiration for much of her work.

Epilogue

"IN CREATING, the only hard thing's to begin," wrote James Russell Lowell. "A grass-blade's no easier to make than an oak;/If you've once found the way, you've achieved the grand stroke." Though for most craftsmen the first step is the most difficult, few find beginning "the only hard thing." Whether you're looking for new scope for seasoned skills or learning a new craft, countless organizations and publications exist to help you.

Listing all the possibilities would require a book in its own right; the following suggestions may ease some of the difficulties.

Talking with practitioners in your field of interest will probably be most helpful of all. They have the experience, and often can anticipate your difficulties before they arise. (Don't be surprised if they disagree on the merits of a how-to-do-it book or manual!) Nearly every town has craftsmen, so local sources should be the first you consult.

Check for courses and workshops offered at the "Y" and other community centers or by schools and nearby colleges. Thousands of craft guilds are active over the nation; local branches or groups can advise you. Also, your public library probably offers many books and periodicals on crafts. Some libraries even have how-to filmstrips.

In addition to local resources, you may find help from other groups.

The American Crafts Council, with regional representatives in many areas, is an outstanding clearinghouse of information—especially for artist-craftsmen. Serving both amateurs and professionals, it publishes *Craft Horizons*, a bimonthly magazine with valuable reviews of current how-to books. It also puts out an annual *Directory of Craft Courses*—available for $4.00—as well as bibliographies on clay, enamel, metal, glass, wood, and fiber. These may be purchased through the Council's Publications Sales Department, 44 West 53rd Street, New York, New York 10019.

Government agencies provide many services for craftsmen. The United States Department of Agriculture sponsors an extensive crafts program, covering a wide variety of subjects, through its Cooperative Extension Service. To find out what it offers in your area, write to Craft Specialist, Craft Development Program, Farmer Cooperative Service, Department of Agriculture, Washington, D. C. 20250.

Cultural Directory: Guide to Federal Funds and Services for Cultural Activities lists many other federally run or funded programs, including those for teachers, veterans, and the handicapped. It sells for $4.00 through Associated Council of the Arts Publications, 1564 Broadway, New York, New York 10036.

Each state maintains a state arts council, and some of these have programs specifically for craftsmen. If yours does not, your requests might prompt them to set one up.

Serious students, especially anyone interested in crafts as a career, should look into *By Hand: A Guide to Schools and Careers in Crafts*, by John Coyne and Tom Hebert. E. P. Dutton & Co. publishes this as a Sunrise paperback for $3.95. The working craftsman will find information on sales outlets in *Contemporary Crafts Market Place*, recently compiled by the American Crafts Council. It may be available in a library; it may be purchased for $13.95, plus 40 cents handling charge, from R. R. Bowker Order Department, Box 1807, Ann Arbor, Michigan 48106.

If you just enjoy looking at craftwork, museums and galleries and fairs are obvious places to start.

Whether you consider yourself an amateur craftsman or a professional, a novice or an old-timer, you can surely find in craftwork a unique appreciation for basic materials and the amazing abilities of human hands. Writing of use and contemplation in this realm, Mexico's distinguished poet Octavio Paz calls craftsmanship "the heartbeat of human time. A thing that is handmade is a useful object but also one that is beautiful. . . ."

Authors' Notes

Reared on an Ozarks farm, CLAY ANDERSON graduated from the University of Missouri, served in the Army, and since 1965 has published the magazine *The Ozarks Mountaineer* in Branson, Mo. He wrote a chapter on the region for Special Publications' 1973 book *American Mountain People,* and one on work for *Life in Rural America* in 1974.

Free-lance writer ANDY LEON HARNEY, a graduate of Goucher College, served as a Peace Corps volunteer in Maharashtra, India, from 1967 to 1970. She specializes in urban ethnic affairs and art, and reviews craft exhibitions in the Washington, D. C., area for *Craft Horizons.*

Before he joined the Society's staff in 1971, TOM MELHAM received his B.S. degree from Cornell and M.A. from the University of Missouri. A city dweller, he makes tables from urban litter like cable spools and cast-off framing.

A native of New York City and graduate of Hunter College, CYNTHIA RUSS RAMSAY grew interested in textiles while living in Iran and in India. Joining the Society's staff in 1966, she has been project editor for two Special Publications, has written chapters for *The Alps* and *Life in Rural America,* and is now managing editor for the Society's children's book program.

As a free-lance writer and editor, PATRICIA L. RAYMER specializes in the contemporary visual arts. Her article "Wisconsin's Menominee Indians" appeared in the August 1974 NATIONAL GEOGRAPHIC, with photographs by her husband, Steve, of the Society's staff. She received her B.A. and M.A. from the University of Wisconsin.

A Virginian by birth, rearing, and residence, BEVERLY SPOTSWOOD brings the insights of a trained child psychologist and the experience of a therapist to the subject of toys and their importance to children.

New Englander C. MALCOLM WATKINS, educated at Harvard University, has been a curator involved with American crafts since 1936. Formerly with Old Sturbridge Village, he joined the staff of the Smithsonian Institution in 1948; he has worked in its Division of Ethnology, and has served as chairman of the Department of Cultural History, where he is now a senior curator.

Acknowledgments

The Special Publications Division is grateful to the individuals, agencies, and organizations named or quoted or portrayed in this book, and to those cited here, for their generous cooperation and help during its preparation: Fritz Dreisbach, Helen Drutt, Nora Fisher, Charles F. Montgomery of Yale University, Eleanor Moty, Caroline C. Ramsay, Richard L. Spivey, Joan Pearson Watkins, Sandra Zimmerman.

In particular, the division extends its thanks to the organizations and the individuals listed below for their courtesy in making objects of craftwork available for illustration. Sam Maloof, Tom McGlauchlin, and Dominick Labino have supplied photographs. Numerous curators and staff members, as well as private collectors, have assisted the following photographers: Lowell Georgia, Shirley Marein, David Doubilet, Donna Grosvenor, Martin Rogers and Kathy Andrisevic, in addition to Jennifer Urquhart, N.G.S. staff, and N.G.S. Photographers Joseph H. Bailey, Victor R. Boswell, Jr., Bruce Dale, Bates Littlehales.

SMITHSONIAN INSTITUTION: p. 16, bed; p. 19, hinges; p. 39, ladderback chair; pp. 44-45, masks; p. 46, kachina doll; p. 47, statue; p. 75, effigy jug; p. 102, blanket, center left; p. 104, Micmac basket, Paiute decoy; p. 105, Pomo baskets.

SHELBURNE MUSEUM, INC., Shelburne, Vermont: p. 6, Indian and mermaid vanes; p. 35, wig stand and mold; p. 37, bowl; p. 38, highchair; p. 55, shop sign; p. 57, mallard and curlew decoys; p. 59, gourd fiddle.

THE HISTORICAL SOCIETY OF YORK COUNTY, York, Pa.: p. 48, Punch; p. 51, Justice; p. 151, Ark and animals; p. 152, doll; p. 156, chair, pitcher and bowl; p. 158, stuffed horse, wooden horse; p. 161, rooster pull toy.

SAN DIEGO MUSEUM OF MAN: p. 4, painting; p. 79, Santo Domingo olla; p. 104, Maidu basket, Panamint basket; p. 105, Makah baskets; pp. 108-109, all items; p. 153, doll.

THE HENRY FRANCIS DU PONT WINTERTHUR MUSEUM, Winterthur, Del.: pp. 16-17, Story room; p. 25, sugar bowl; p. 38, Duncan Phyfe chair; p. 39, Windsor chair; p. 43, high chest; p. 54, Schimmel eagle; p. 97, bed covering; p. 112, needlework picture.

PHILADELPHIA MUSEUM OF ART: p. 25, Stiegel-type tumbler, purchased: Special Museum Fund; p. 42, schrank, purchased; p. 43, Empire secretary (detail), given by Mr. and Mrs. Edward C. Page in memory of Robert E. Griffith; p. 79, dish, given by John T. Morris; p. 91, coffeepot, purchased: the John D. McIlhenny Fund; p. 110, sampler, the Whitman Sampler Collection, given by Pet Incorporated.

THE MUSEUM OF FINE ARTS, Boston: p. 26, detail, *Creole* figurehead; p. 42, chest; p. 54, desk inlay; p. 88, all items—portrait, gift of Joseph W., William B., and Edward H. R. Revere; p. 88, teapot; p. 90, sugar box, teapot.

AMERICAN ANTIQUARIAN SOCIETY: p. 16, p. 19, p. 25, engravings, *The Book of Trades* (1807); p. 67, trade card (detail).

Collection of Ken Deavers & Ed Nash, THE AMERICAN HAND: p. 84, vase; p. 85, teapot; p. 182, teapot.

THE ESSEX INSTITUTE, Salem, Mass.: p. 63, model; p. 118, Lucy Cleveland quilting bee; p. 154, wooden-head doll, nut-head doll.

NANTUCKET HISTORICAL ASSOCIATION: p. 68, "sailor's valentine"; p. 70, scrimshaw, all items; p. 71, pie crimper; p. 107, nested baskets.

ABBY ALDRICH ROCKEFELLER FOLK ART COLLECTION: p. 6, snake vane; p. 89, tinsmith's sign; p. 110, embroidered picture by Mary Rees; p. 158, "Boy in Plaid."

NATIONAL GALLERY OF ART, Washington, D. C.: p. 15, "Flax Scutching Bee," by Linton Park; gift of Edgar William and Bernice Chrysler Garbisch; p. 97, hooked rug (eagle), p. 101, homespun, p. 115, crocheted doily, 1875, all from the Index of American Design.

NEW YORK PUBLIC LIBRARY: p. 33, p. 75, p. 101, engravings by Alexander Anderson, all from the Prints Division: Astor, Lenox and Tilden Foundations.

THE PILGRIM SOCIETY, Plymouth, Mass.: p. 36, mortar and pestle; p. 37, grain measure; p. 38, Brewster chair.

SAN FRANCISCO MARITIME MUSEUM: p. 55, eagle from steamboat *Brother Jonathan;* p. 66, p. 67, figureheads.

THE BALTIMORE MUSEUM OF ART: p. 116, album quilt (detail), gift of the Women's Board of Managers of the Wesley Home, Inc.; pp. 116-117, album quilt, gift of Dr. William Rush Dunton, Jr.

THE ENCHANTED DOLL HOUSE, Manchester Center, Vermont: p. 154, "Victorian" rag doll; p. 156, composite room.

CIRCUS WORLD MUSEUM, Baraboo, Wisconsin: p. 53, wagon panel; p. 55, wagon eagle.

HANCOCK SHAKER VILLAGE, Hancock, Mass.: p. 39, Shaker chair; p. 40, Shaker room.

OHIO HISTORICAL SOCIETY: front endpaper, quilt; p. 11, engraving.

OLD STURBRIDGE VILLAGE, Sturbridge, Mass.: p. 75, redware—green jug, red jar with lid.

MYSTIC SEAPORT, INC., Mystic, Conn.: p. 26, figurehead, *Great Admiral,* courtesy of Sumner Pingree, Jr., Charles Weld Pingree, John R. Pingree, p. 69, macramé.

NEW YORK STATE HISTORICAL ASSOCIATION, Cooperstown: p. 48, Indian woman; p. 49, "Jim Crow."

P. 4, peace medal, from a private collection.

P. 25, Tiffany window, Helga Studio photo courtesy the magazine *Antiques,* collection of Dr. and Mrs. Robert Koch.

P. 31, flag gate, MUSEUM OF AMERICAN FOLK ART, New York City; Welton gate, THE MATTATUCK MUSEUM, Waterbury, Conn.

P. 38, Thomas Day chair, Mrs. Stanley C. Harrell, Durham, N.C.

P. 40, Victorian room, THE ILLINOIS STATE MUSEUM, courtesy Ethel P. Black.

P. 48, cigar-store Indian, THE PENNSYLVANIA FARM MUSEUM OF LANDIS VALLEY, Lancaster, Pa.

P. 51, statue (detail) by William Rush, the Fairmount Park Commission and the PHILADELPHIA MUSEUM OF ART; bootmaker's trade figure, EVERHART MUSEUM, Scranton, Pa.

P. 54, banjo eagle, Marshall L. Founds, Chestertown, Md.

P. 56, passenger pigeon decoy, Mrs. Ed C. Sterling, Randolph, Vt.

P. 68, crewelwork, collection of Mr. and Mrs. Sydney Jacoff.

P. 71, "Victorian lady" scrimshaw, collection of J. R. A.

P. 75, stoneware jug, collection of Mr. and Mrs. A. Christian Revi.

P. 76, flag, the NEW-YORK HISTORICAL SOCIETY, New York City.

P. 89, coffeepot, private collection of Herbert R. Collins.

P. 90, pitcher, collection of THE ART INSTITUTE OF CHICAGO (accession no. 1973. 357), gift of Raymond W. Sheets.

P. 99, quilt, "Blue Traditions," Mrs. Morton C. Katzenberg.

P. 102, Navajo rug (lower left), THE INDIAN CRAFT SHOP, U. S. Department of the Interior, Washington, D. C.

P. 107, collection of 8 baskets (top), Gwen Gaillard.

P. 119, quilt top, Mrs. Ed C. Sterling.

P. 120, Broken Star quilt, the Frances Knight Silcott family.

P. 121, Amish quilt, Renee Butler.

P. 127, owl, QUALLA ARTS & CRAFTS MUTUAL, INC., Cherokee, N. C.

P. 155, Raggedy Ann, by Ramona, THIS OLD HOUSE CRAFTS, Rising Fawn, Ga.; applehead doll, MIRACLE'S MOUNTAIN CRAFTS, Middlesboro, Ky.

P. 159, pull toy, Dudley Littlehales.

P. 161, clothespin doll and horse, Velton Searcy, Hendersonville, N.C.

P. 186, top left, bottom center, bottom right, Baron Wolman (Levi Strauss & Co.), upper right, bottom left, Levi Strauss & Co.

P. 190, shell necklace, SEALS AND OWLS, Carmel, Calif.

Index

Boldface indicates illustrations; *italic* refers to picture captions

Adams, Arlie 125, 126
Adobe houses **11, 22**
Adrosko, Rita J. 94
Afro-American crafts **75,** 172, **175,** *189*
Albertson, Eric: carvings **50**
Allanstand Shop, Asheville, N.C. 129
Althoz, David **157**
Amelung, Johann Friedrich 24
American Crafts Council 194
Amish: barn-raisings 18, **20-21;** quilts 98, **121**
Anderson, John: figurehead **26**
Appalachia 124-149; broom-makers 128, **148-149;** chairmakers 124, 133-134, **137, 142-143;** instrument-makers 124, 125, **125, 146-147;** potters 132, **144-145;** quilting **95,** 134, 135, **139;** quilts **120-121;** textiles 94, 96-99, **99,** 101, **138;** toys 129-130, *129,* 135, **137,** 151, **155, 160-161;** weavers 94, 96, **100,** 130, 131; woodwork 126, **126,** 128, 129, *129,* 134-135, carvers 126, *127,* **133,** cooper **140-141**
Apprentices: colonial 13, 74; contemporary 170, **189**
Arneson, Robert **183**
Arquero, Juanita C. 72, **80**
Arrowmont School of Crafts, Gatlinburg, Tenn. 128, 130
Artist-craftsmen 24-25, 164-193
Arts and crafts movement (1876-1916) 24, *90,* 167

Bahr, Rudolf P. **173**
Barka, Norman 74
Barn-raisings 18, **20-21**
Barrington, Lynn **139**
Bartels, William: table **40**
Basketmakers **104, 106, 138, 175, 189**
Baskets 12; bone **70;** Indian **104-105,** beaded **109;** miniature **104, 105;** Nantucket lightship **106-107**
Beadwork, Indian **108-109**
Bedspread 99, **99**
Begay, Mary **102**
Bennett, Mary Jane **175**
Berea College, Berea, Ky. 130, *160*
Berger, Clarence **59**
Bishop Hill, Ill.: blacksmith 75, **86, 87**
Blacksmiths: contemporary 75-76, **86, 87,** 126, **184-185;** Early American *14,* **19,** 22, 23, 75, 76
Blackware 10, **84, 167**

Blair, Arlinka 5; wall hanging **122-123**
Blair, Dee 125-126, 134
Blair, Everett 124
Blair, Hobart: carving **150**
Blair, Preston 124, **125**
Blankets, Navajo **102, 103**
Boardman & Hart: teapot **88**
Boat building **189**
Bowls: silver **77,** 78; wooden 10, **36-37, 41, 133**
Boyd, E. 14
Broom-making 13, 128, **148-149**
Brown, Bill 130
Buhler, Kathryn C. 77
Bushnell, R. E. **3,** *42*
Bybee Pottery, Bybee, Ky. 132, **144-145**

Cabinetmakers **3,** 28, 30, **42, 178-179;** Early American **16,** *17,* 23, 24, 28, *38, 43, 51; see also* Chairmakers
Carpenter, Arthur (Espenet) **179**
Carpentry 18, 19; barn-raising **20-21;** house-raising **11**
Carrousel figures 32, 34, **52**
Carving *see* Scrimshaw; Toys; Woodcarving
Castle, Wendell **178**
Centennial Exposition, Philadelphia 24, 166, 172
Ceramics: dolls **162;** *see also* Pottery
Cernigliaro, Salvatore 34
Chairmakers 23, *38,* **39,** 124, 133-134, **137, 142-143**
Chairs 124, 133-134, **137, 142-143, 178, 179;** Early American 23, **38-39;** miniature **156;** Shaker 28, **39, 40**
Charles F. Crocker (barkentine): figurehead **67**
Charles W. Morgan (whaler) 31
Cherokee Indians: basketmaking **104**
Chippewa Indians: beadwork **108**
Churns **140, 141**
Cigar-store Indians 34, **48**
Circus-wagon carvings **53, 55**
Circus World Museum, Baraboo, Wis. *53*
Clark, Bruce 166
Clark, Margaret Haass 99; needle-point **112-113**
Cochiti Pueblo, N. Mex.: potters 10, 72, **80**

Coffeepots: silver **91;** tinware **89**
Colonial Williamsburg, Va.: instru-ment-maker 34, **58;** silversmith 78, **92-93**
Colwell, Ken 173
Comanche pipe pouch **109**
Coney, John 78; sugar box **90**
Conn, Miki **189**
Cook, Bertha 98-99, **99**
Cooper **140-141**
Copley, John Singleton: Revere portrait 13, **77,** 78
Copp, Jonathan: "great chair" 23, **39**
Copperwork **77,** 78; kitchenware 166, **184;** weather vane **7**
Copple, Sharon: woodcarving **135**
Corbitt, Gretchen **146**
Cordero, Helen 10, 12
Cornelison, Walter: pottery 132, **144-145**
Cornshuck dolls 129-130, **155**
Counts, Charles 72, **73,** 74, 78
Coverlets, woven 94, 96, **97;** patterns 96, 131, Lover's Knot **101,** Walls of Jericho 94, **100-101**
Craft demonstrations and exhibits **8-9,** 10, **31,** *37,* **79,** 135, *186 see also* Bishop Hill, Ill.; Colonial Williamsburg, Va.; Mystic Seaport, Conn.; Old Sturbridge Village, Mass.; Salem College, W. Va.
Craft fairs 126, 131, 166
Craft guilds and societies: contem-porary 98, 128, 130, 131, 166, 194; Early American **76,** 77
Craft instruction 128, 129, 130, 167, 171, 172-173, 194; Schools: Appa-lachian State University, N.C. *147;* Berea College 130, *160;* California State University, Long Beach *165;* Cranbrook Academy of Art 174; Fiberworks 173; Haystack Moun-tain School of Crafts 172, **189;** Penland School of Crafts 130, 172, **188;** Salem College **118, 136-139;** University of Wisconsin-Madison 170, 171
Crafts movement, contemporary 24, 166-167, 172
Craftsmen: colonial terms for 13; social and economic roles 10, 13-14, 22-25, 74, 75, 76, 77, 94, 124, 134, 165, 166-167, 170, 171, 172, women's 23, 172; *see also* Apprentices; Artist-craftsmen; Folk-craftsmen; Indentured servants; Journeymen; Master craftsmen; Slave-craftsmen
The Craftsmen of Chelsea Court, Washington, D. C. 170
Cranbrook Academy of Art, Bloom-field Hills, Mich. 174
Creole (packet): figurehead **26**
Crewelwork **68, 111, 116**
Crochet **114-115,** 180
Cross, Helena Barnett 130-131
Crow Indians: beadwork **108**

Cummings, Frank **165;** craftwork **165, 191**
Curtis, James 78, **92-93**

Da, Tony 72
David Crockett (clipper): carving **66**
Davidson, Mary Frances 97
Day, Thomas 24; chair **38**
Decoys **56-57, 104**
Dennis, Thomas *17;* chest **42**
Dentzel, Gustav 32, 34
Deschamps, May Ritchie 129, **155**
Doll houses 151, **157;** furniture **156**
Dollmakers **46, 155, 162-163**
Dolls 108, 118, 150-151, **152-155, 162-163;** apple-headed **155;** ceramic **162;** cornshuck 129-130, **155;** kachina dolls **46,** 150; nut-headed **118, 154;** rag 150, **152, 154, 155;** stomper dolls **137,** 151; wooden 150, **154, 163**
Drowne, Shem 76; weather vane **7**
Dyeing, textiles 96-97, *97,* 172, 173

Eagles *see* Patriotic motifs
Eames, Charles 78
Edaville Railroad Museum, South Carver, Mass. *63*
Embroidery 67, **97,** 98, **110, 111, 186;** crewelwork **68, 111, 116;** samplers 98, **110**
Engler, Peter 132
Enlow, Harold: whittling **29, 135**
Erlacher, Max *169*
Espenet (Arthur Carpenter) **179**
Everist, Mary: quilt **116-117**

Fahnstrom, Stewart 75-76, **86, 87**
Farragut, David: figurehead of **26**
Farriers *14,* 75, 76
Fenster, Fred 166
Fenton Art Glass Company, Williamstown, W. Va. **168-169;** open house 171-172
Ferrian, Marie **162, 163**
Fiber *9,* 94-123, 164, 165, 172-173; Early American 22, 94-97, **97, 101;** *see also* Baskets; Coverlets; Fiber sculpture; Needlework; Quilts; Weaving
Fiber sculpture *68, 115,* 164, **167, 180-181, 187**
Fiberworks (school), Berkeley, Calif. 173
Figureheads **26-27,** 32, **66, 67**
Fisch, Arline **193;** jewelry **192, 193**
Fisher, John: statue 51
Flax 96; scutching bee **14-15**
Folk-craftsmen 14, 18 *see also* Appalachia; Ozarks
Foot, Mary: bed covering **97**
Fort New Salem, W. Va. *see* Salem College
Funk art **183**
Furniture **16-17,** 23, 28, 30, **38-43, 137, 142-143, 156, 178-179** *see also* Cabinetmakers; Chairmakers

Gates: iron *184;* wooden **31**
Gay Head (whaler): scrimshaw **71**
Gieling, Imogene: silverwork **90, 191**
Gilkerson, William: scrimshaw **71**
Glass: blown **25, 168-169,** 170-172, enameled **25;** stained **25, 176**
Glass Art Society (GAS) 166, 171-172
Glassblowers 24, **25, 168-169,** 170-171
Gold **190-191**
Goldsmiths **77;** society 166
Gooch, William 74
Goodman, Ron 180
Goodwin Guild (weavers) 131
Grayson, Persis 96, 99
Great Admiral (clipper): figurehead **26**
Greer, Taft 94, 96, **100**
Grider, Jakey 128-129
Grier, Rosey 172
Gronborg, Erik 166, **182**
Gruelle, Johnny *154*
Guns 76, 134, **173**

Hageman, Rita: crochet **115**
Harral, Rex 126, 128
Haystack Mountain School of Crafts, Deer Isle, Maine 172, **189**
Hensley, Bea **185**
Hensley, Oscar 132-133
Heritage Plantation, Cape Cod, Mass. 34
Hicks, Stanley **147**
Higgins, Josie 97-98
Hindman settlement school, Ky. 130
Hinges **19,** 23, back endpaper
Hitchcock chair, miniature **156**
Hoffa, Bob 30
Holstein, Jonathan 98
Homespun **101**
Hopi Indians: jewelry *192;* kachina dolls **46,** 150; pottery **79, 80**
Hostetler, David 5, **65;** sculpture **64**
Houses: colonial **11, 16-17,** 18-19, 22; contemporary 174-175, **176-177**
Howarth, James 174
Hubbell, J. Lorenzo *103*
Hubbell, James: home 174-175, **176-177**
Hubbell Trading Post, Ganado, Ariz. **102-103**

Indentured servants 23, 24
Indian crafts **4,** 10, **11,** 12, 172; basketry **104-105, 109;** beadwork **108-109;** decoys 56, **104;** dolls **153,** apple-headed *154,* kachina dolls **46,** 150; jewelry **190, 192;** pottery 10, 72, **79, 80, 84,** *167;* weaving **102-103;** woodcarving **36, 44-45, 46,** 150
Industrial Revolution *9,* 22
Ink, Jack 168
Iron Mountain Stoneware, Inc., Laurel Bloomery, Tenn. 72, 75
Ironwork **15, 87,** *184;* hinges **19,** 23, back endpaper; weather vanes **6-7, 185;** *see also* Blacksmiths

Iroquois Indians: ceremonial mask **45;** dolls *154*

Jarvie, Robert R.: silver pitcher **90**
Jarvis, Henry B. 31-32
Jenness, Kevin 88
Jerry, Michael 75, 76, 77; saucepan **184**
Jewelry 166, 170, **190-193;** mourning ring **77;** wooden 129
John C. Campbell Folk School, Brasstown, N.C. 129, 130
Journeymen 13

Kachina dolls **46,** 150
Kear, Elmer 128, **148-149**
Kear, Omah 128, *149*
Kilns 74, 76, **81, 82-83,** 132, **145, 162**
Kington, Brent **185**
Klamath Indians: beaded basket **109**
Klene, Cecilia **9**
Knotwork 67, **69**
Kovach, Mrs. Ivan 138

Labino, Dominick 171; glass sculpture **169**
Laky, Gyöngy (Ginger) 173
Lang, Rodger 166
Langlet, Ragnhild 123
Leafgreen, Harvey 171
Lechtzin, Stanley: jewelry **190**
Ledford, Virgil: woodcarving **127**
Lees, Albert 89
Lévi-Strauss, Claude 94
Levi Strauss & Co.: Denim Art Contest entries **186**
Lewis, Madeline 189
Limberjack **137**
Littlehales, Dorothy: crewelwork **111**
Littleton, Harvey **168,** 170-171
Log cabins *11,* 22; "raising" **11**
Loloma, Charles **192**
Looff, Charles 34
Looms **8-9,** 94, **100-101, 188;** museum 173; Navajo **102-103**
Lyman, Henry Hawkins, Jr.: teapot **85**

McGlauchlin, Tom **168,** 171
McKay, Donald **8**
McNeill, J. R.: violin **59**
Maidu (Indian) basket **104**
Makah Indians: baskets **105**
Maloof, Sam 23, 25, **39,** *53;* furniture **39, 41**
Martinez, Apolonio 18
Martinez, Julian 10, *167*
Martinez, Maria 10, 72, **167**
Masks: Indian ceremonial **44-45**
Mass production: effects on craft traditions 12, 13, 24, 34, *53,* 96, 151, *159,* 170, 172
Master craftsmen: colonial 13
Matthews, Rufus **79**
Means, Mrs. Fred **139**
Merritt, Francis 172
Metalwork **6-7,** 75-78, **77, 86-93,** *167,* 170, 174, **184-185** *see also* Blacksmiths; Jewelers; Pewterers; Silversmiths; Tinsmiths

Additional Reading

GENERAL: Carl Bridenbaugh, *The Colonial Craftsman;* Marshall B. Davidson, *The American Heritage History of Colonial Antiques;* Jean Lipman and Alice Winchester, *The Flowering of American Folk Art;* CONTEMPORARY: Mildred Constantine and Jack Lenor Larsen, *Beyond Craft: the Art Fabric;* Charles Counts, *Encouraging American Craftsmen;* Lee Nordness, *Objects: U S A.* SPECIFIC AREAS OR PERIODS: E. Boyd, *Popular Arts of Spanish New Mexico;* Robert Judson Clark, editor, *The Arts and Crafts Movement in America 1876-1916;* Allen H. Eaton, *Handicrafts of the Southern Highlands;* Betty I. Madden, *Art, Crafts, and Architecture in Early Illinois;* INDIAN: Frederick J. Dockstader, *Indian Art in America;* Frederic H. Douglas, editor, Indian Leaflet Series, Denver Art Museum; Emma Lila Fundaburk, *Sun Circles and Human Hands;* Mary Hunt Kahlenberg and Anthony Berlant, *The Navajo Blanket;* Otis Tufton Mason, *Aboriginal American Basketry;* Clara Lee Tanner, *Southwest Indian Craft Arts.* SPECIFIC CRAFTS: Wood: Edward Deming Andrews and Faith Andrews, *Religion in Wood, A Book of Shaker Furniture;* Joel Barber, *Wild Fowl Decoys;* M. V. Brewington, *Shipcarvers of North America;* Frederick Fried, *Artists in Wood;* Eric Sloane, *A Reverence for Wood;* Pottery: Edwin Atlee Barber, *Tulip Ware of the Pennsylvania-German Potters;* John Bivins, Jr., *The Moravian Potters in North Carolina;* Lura Woodside Watkins, *Early New England Potters and Their Wares;* Metal: Martha Gandy Fales, *Early American Silver;* Charles F. Montgomery, *A History of American Pewter;* Margaret Coffin, *American Country Tinware 1700-1900;* Textiles: Rita J. Adrosko, *Natural Dyes and Home Dyeing;* Mary Meigs Atwater, *The Shuttle-craft Book of American Hand-Weaving;* Mary Frances Davidson, *The Dye-Pot;* Jonathan Holstein, *The Pieced Quilt;* Patsy and Myron Orlofsky, *Quilts in America;* Hope Hanley, *Needlepoint in America;* Shirley Marein, *Stitchery, Needlepoint, Appliqué and Patchwork: A Complete Guide;* Ed Rossbach, *Baskets as Textile Art;* Clifford W. Ashley, *The Ashley Book of Knots;* Glass: Robert Koch, *Louis C. Tiffany, Rebel in Glass;* Helen and George S. McKearin, *Two Hundred Years of American Blown Glass.* MISCELLANEOUS: Eliot Wigginton, editor, *Foxfire 1* and 2.

Micmac Indians: basket, miniature **104**
Miera y Pacheco, Bernardo 14; carving **47**
Mimbres culture: pottery 10
Miracle, Hazel: woodcraft **126**
Models and miniatures 125-126; baskets **104, 105;** covered wagon **160;** furniture **156;** locomotive **62-63;** ships **60-61**
Mondragón, José 18, **47**
Monroe, Robert **189**
Morgan, Lucy 130
Museum of New Mexico, Santa Fe *189*
Museum of the American Indian, Heye Foundation, New York City 10
Musical instruments 34; banjos 124, 125, **125, 147;** dulcimers *133,* **146-147;** violins 34-35, **58-59**
Mystic Seaport, Conn. 31; ship carver 24, **27**

Nakashima, George 28, 30
Nampeyo, Rachael **80**
Nantucket lightship baskets **106-107**
Naranjo, Elizabeth: pottery **84**
Navajos: rugmaking **102-103;** silverwork 12
Needlepoint 99, **112-113,** 172
Needlework 67, 97-99, **99, 122-123,** 186; crochet **114-115;** embroidery **68,** 97, **110-111;** needlepoint 99, **112-113,** 172; *see also* Quilts

New York Society of Pewterers: banner **76,** 77
Nicholson, Oral **138**
Noah's Ark (toy) 150, **150-151**
Noël Hume, Ivor 74
Norton, James C.: locomotive, scale model **62-63**
Nyburg, Mary **81, 82**
Nygaard, Marsha **187**

Old Salem, N.C.: potter **79**
Old Sturbridge Village, Mass. 10, **15;** cabinetmaker **2-3, 42;** pewterer **88;** tinsmith **89**
Owl (woodcarving) **127**
Ozark Arts & Crafts Fair, War Eagle, Ark. **131**
Ozarks 124, *125,* 126, 128, 130-131, 134; carving **150;** musical instruments **59,** 124, **125;** weavers 131; whittling **29;** woodcarvers 132, *135;* woodcarvings **135**

Paiute (Indian) decoy **104**
Paley, Albert **184;** necklace **191°**
Panamint (Indian) basket **104**
Parsons, Deborah 130, 131
Patriotic motifs **1,** 23, **26-27, 31, 35, 54-55, 67, 97, 186**
Peach-pit toys 150, **150**
Peacock, zinc **89**
Pearson, Ronald Hayes 167, 170; necklace **190**
Peck, Tildy: quilts **95, 121**

Penland School of Crafts, N.C. 130, 172, **188**
Pennsylvania Germans 23; furniture **42;** pottery 74, **79,** *156;* toys **161;** *see also* Amish
Pewter 76-77, **88**
Pewterers 77, **88;** New York City society banner **76,** 77
Phillips, John Marshall 13
Phyfe, Duncan: chair 28, **38**
Picchi, Cindy: crochet **114-115**
Pinder, Mrs. Clayton **139**
Pine Mountain settlement school, Ky. 130
Pitchers: pottery **73, 144, 145, 156;** silver 78, **90**
Pomo Indians: baskets **105**
Posilkin, Ellen Reiben 170
Potters 72, **73, 75, 79,** 80, 81, 82, *84,* 132, **144, 182, 183;** colonial American 23, 72, 74-75; Indian 10, 12, 72, **79,** 80, *84,* **167;** Pennsylvania German 74, *79, 156*
Potter's wheel 12, 74, **75, 79, 144;** jigger wheel **145**
Pottery 72-75, **73, 79-85, 144-145, 156, 167, 182, 183, 189;** firing 72, 74, 75, **80, 82-83,** *84;* glazes 75, **75,** *81, 84,* 132, *182;* Indian 10, 72, **79,** 80, 84, **167;** techniques: coiling 72, **79,** *84,* **189,** throwing **73,** 74, **75, 79;** types: earthenware 74, **75, 79,** porcelain **85,** stoneware 75, **75,** 81
Presnell, Edd **133;** woodwork **126, 133**

Quilting 95, 97-98, 134, 135, **139;** styles 98, **99,** *116, 118*
Quilting bees 98, *116*
Quilts front endpaper; album quilt **116-117;** contemporary **122;** crazy quilt top **118-119;** friendship quilts *116;* patterns 95, 135, Broken Star **120,** Double Wedding Ring **121,** Field Daisy **121,** Grandmother's Flower Garden **95,** Log Cabin **120,** Monkey Wrench **120,** Split Rail **139,** Sunshine and Shadow **121**

Radakovich, Svetozar: necklace **190**
Revere, Paul 13, 78, *90;* portrait 13, **77,** 78
Reyes, José F. **106**
Ritchie, Abigail Hall 130
Ritchie, Mallie 130
Rogers, William ("the Poor Potter") 74, 75
Ronnberg, Erik, Jr. **61**
Rookwood Pottery, Cincinnati, Ohio 24
Ropework 67, **69**
Rouse, Harold **175**
Rugs: hooked **97;** Navajo **102-103**
Rush, William: statue **51**
Rust, Milton D. **173**

Saddler **173**
Sailors' crafts 66-67, **68-71**

Salem College, Salem, W. Va.: heritage arts program **118, 136-139**

Samplers 98, **110**

San Francisco Maritime Museum, Calif.: ship's carvings **66, 67**

San Ildefonso Pueblo, N. Mex.: pottery 10, 72, **167**

Santa Clara Pueblo, N. Mex.: pottery 84

Santo Domingo Pueblo, N. Mex.: jewelry **190**; pottery **79**

santos ("saints") 150, 175; carvers of 14, 18, **47**

Sauceboat, silver **92-93**

Schimmel, Wilhelm *55*, 151; woodcarving **54-55**

School of the Ozarks, Point Lookout, Mo. 130

Scrimshaw 67, **70-71**

Sculpture: glass **168, 169** *see also* Fiber sculpture; Woodcarvings

Sekimachi, Kay **181**

Seth Story house, Essex, Mass. 18, 19, 22; museum exhibits **16-17**

Shaker furniture 28, **40**; chair 28, **39**

Shawcroft, Barbara **181**

Shepard, Willard 24, **27**

Ship carvers 24, **27**, 66; trade card **67**

Ship models **60-61**

Ship's carvings **26-27, 55**, 66, **66, 67**

Shipwrights 10, 30-32, 66

Shop signs 34, **51**, *53*, **55, 89**; cigar-store Indians 48

Short, Mrs. Charles **118**

Shoshone Indians: doll 153

Silcott, Frances Knight: quilt **120**

Silversmiths 78, *90*, **92-93**; Early American *51*, 77-78, *90 see also* Revere, Paul

Silverwork **4**, 77, **90-91, 92-93, 190-192**; Indian 12, *192*

Singleton, Kitty Ritchie 130

Slave-craftsmen 24, *48*, 75

Smithsonian Institution, Washington, D. C. 10, 14, 94, *184;* National Museum of History and Technology 12, **16**, 22

Society of North American Goldsmiths (SNAG) 166

Sons of Liberty: Revere punchbowl **77**, 78

Southern Highland Handicraft Guild 128, 130, 131; craft fairs 131

Spinner, David: pottery **79**

Spinning 96, **102, 138**; spinning wheels 12, **101**

Spoons: pewter 77, **88**; wooden 126, 128

Stained glass **25, 176**

Stamper, Lottie **104**

Steelman, Bonnie: quilt **121**

Stewart, Alex **140, 141**

Stiegel, Henry William *25*

"Stiegel-type" glassware **25**

Stocksdale, Bob **36**, *40*

Stomper dolls **137**, 151

Storer, Maria Longworth Nichols 24

Story, Seth: house *17*, 18, 19, 22

Sugar bowl, glass **25**

Sugar box, silver **90**

Sully Plantation, Va.: weaving demonstration **8-9**

Syng, Philip, Jr.: silver coffeepot **91**

Tawney, Lenore 164, **167**

Taylor, Janet **188**

Teakettle, silver **90**

Teapots **182**; Britannia **88**; porcelain **85**

Textiles *see* Fiber

Thallmayer, William **1**, *4*

Thomas, Richard 174

Tiffany, Louis Comfort 24, *25;* stained glass **25**

Tinsmiths **89**; colonial American *7*, 76, shop sign **89**

Tinware coffeepot **89**

Tlingit Indians: ceremonial mask **44**

Toledo Museum of Art, Ohio 171

Toys **108**, *129*, 135, **137**, 150-151, **150-163** *see also* Dolls

Tracy, Jared: shellcraft 68

Trains: model **62-63**; toy **160-161**

Treenware 37

Turkey calls 134

University of Wisconsin-Madison 166, 170, 171

Vases: glass **168**; pottery 84

Wall hangings **122-123** *see also* Fiber sculpture

Ward, Lem and Steve: decoys **56-57**

Watson, Ora 134-135; quilts **120**

Watson, Willard **129**, 134-135, **160**

Weather vanes **6-7**, 76, **185**

Weaver, Jerome **137**

Weavers **9**, 24, 94, **100**, 130-131, 164, **167, 181, 188**; Early American 22, 23, 94, 96, **101**; Navajo **102-103**

Weaving **8-9, 100-101**, 130, 131, 173, **181, 188** *see also* Baskets; Fiber sculpture

Wells, James 174

Westphal, Katherine: textiles **122**

Wheelwrights 30

Whimmydiddles 151, **160**

Whitney Museum of American Art, New York City: folk art exhibit *31*

Whittling 28, **29**, *56*, 66, 125, 151; peach pits 150, **150**

Williamsburg, Va. *see* Colonial Williamsburg

Wilson, George D. 34-35, **58**

Windsor chairs 23, **39**

Winston, Leo 174

Winterthur Museum (Henry Francis du Pont Winterthur Museum), Winterthur, Del.: Seth Story house **16-17**, 22

Wistar, Caspar: glass factory 25

Woell, J. Fred 166

Woodcarvers 14, 18, 24, **27**, 32, 34, *43*, **46, 47**, *51*, *53*, *55*, **56, 61**, 63, **65**, *127*, **129, 133, 160, 163**

Woodcarvings **35, 44-57, 60-65, 126-127, 135, 177**; carrousel figures 32, 34, **52**; cigar-store Indians 34, 48; circus wagons **53**, **55**; decoys **56-57**; eagle motif **1**, **26-27, 54-55**, 67; figureheads **26-27**, 32, 67; furniture **40, 42, 43**; gate **31**; kachina dolls **46**, 150; masks **44-45**; *santos* 14, 18, **47**; ships **26-27, 55**, 66, **66, 67**; shop signs 34, 48, **51**, *53*, **55**; toys *129*, 135, **137, 150-151, 154, 158-161**, *162; weather vane* **6**; *see also* Whittling

Woodenware 10, **35, 36-37, 41**, 126, 128-129, **133, 134, 140-141**; Early American **37**; Indian 10, **36**

Woodward, Harry 30

Woodworking 28-65, 66; model-making **61**, *63;* tools **2-3**, 12, 30, 32, **33, 36-37**, 128, **133, 140-141, 142**; *see also* Cabinetmakers; Carpentry; Chairmakers; Cooper; Ship carvers; Woodcarvers

Woody, Arval and Walter 133-134, **142-143**

World Crafts Council: 1974 exhibition, Toronto 10

World's Fair, Chicago 130

Yoke, ox **15**

Yorktown, Va.: pottery 74

Zinc peacock **89**

Zuni Indians 14; kachina dolls 150

Library of Congress CIP Data

National Geographic Society, Washington, D. C. Special Publications Division.
    The craftsman in America.
    1. Handicraft—United States.
    2. Artisans—United States. I. Title.
TT23.N37 1975   680   74-28804
ISBN 0-87044-176-0

Composition for *The Craftsman in America* by National Geographic's Phototypographic Division, Carl M. Shrader, Chief; Lawrence F. Ludwig, Assistant Chief. Printed and bound by Fawcett Printing Corp., Rockville, Md. Color separations by Progressive Color Corp., Rockville, Md.; Graphic Color Plate, Inc., Stamford, Conn.; Colorgraphics, Inc., Beltsville, Md.; and J. Wm. Reed Co., Alexandria, Va.

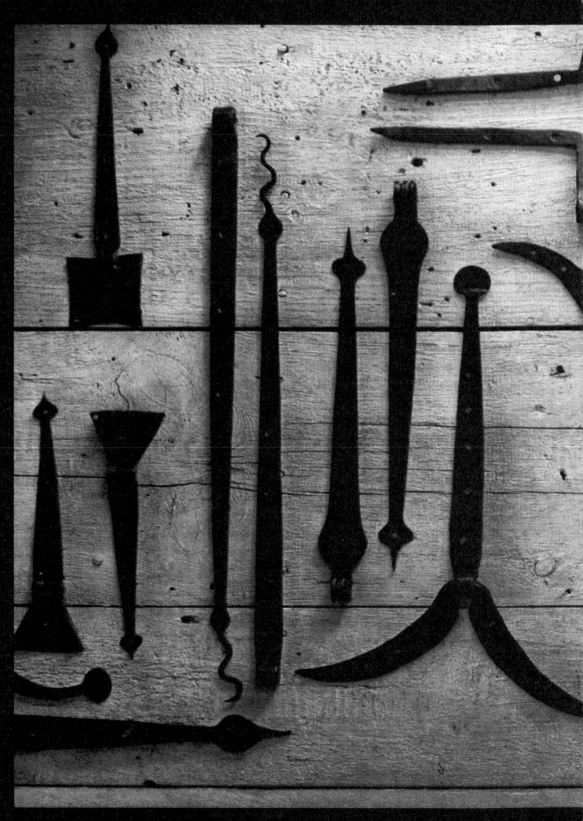

Handwrought iron hinges—for cupboards, chests, shutters, and